# *Accelerando!*

A musical term in Latin that means
"speed up the music!"

# BUILDING WORSHIP BRIDGES

## Accelerating neighborhood connections through worship

**Cathy Townley**

**Kay Kotan**

**Bishop Robert Farr**

Market Square BOOKS

## *Building Worship Bridges*

*Accelerating Neighborhood Connections Through Worship*

books@marketsquarebooks.com
P.O. Box 23664  Knoxville, Tennessee 37933


ISBN: 978-0-9987546-7-3

Library of Congress: 2017961034

Printed and Bound in the United States of America

# Table of Contents

**Part One: Bridging the Worship Gap**

**Part Two: Five Phases of** *Building Worship Bridges*

**The Ten Construction Principles**

# Acknowledgements _____

We are grateful to the many churches we've worked with in our 70 plus years of collective ministry in the field. We have met many people that are devoted to God and to the church. They want to see the church endure and they hope for new people to be transformed by Jesus. Thank you all for teaching us so much.

Many, many thanks also to the congregations and conferences who have been willing to tackle and attempt to improve our local church worship experiences. Thanks to the lay leaders and pastors who see the possibilities of reaching newer, younger and more diverse people through enduring the hard work of changing our worship practices, knowing how important that is for making Sunday worship meaningful to a new generation.

Cathy shouts out to her dear husband, Terry (AKA Mr. T). God definitely put us together, Mr. T. It would not be possible to do this work without your support, your deep understanding of what I do, your insights that always help me, and your constant prayers for me. And now that I'm done writing, I can't wait to go play some golf with you!

Kay wants to extend thanks and appreciation to her husband, Bob, and son, Cameron, for their support of her work, writing, and travel. Their unrelenting encouragement has been both inspiring and priceless for this unconventional ministry.

As always, Bishop Farr thanks his Conference support staff as well as the laity and pastors across Missouri. And thanks to my wife, Susan Farr, for putting up with all my travel around the connection teaching and learning new things.

# Endorsements

"In *Building Worship Bridges*, Cathy Townley, Kay Kotan and Bishop Robert Farr offer intensely practical advice for pastors and church leaders who are on a mission to make the local church worship experience as effective and impactful as possible. I recommend church leaders read this and seek to improve their worship experiences where necessary."

**Ed Stetzer,** *www.edstetzer.com*

"Despite any bluster you may have heard to the contrary, worship services are still the major gateway through which Americans check out the Christian faith and the major means by which they answer the question 'Is this place and this stuff relevant to my life?' You hold in your hands a playbook, crafted by seasoned worship coaches, that will help you    create engaging worship experiences - that will grow human beings and faith communities in your zip code."

**Paul Nixon and BethAnn Estock,** *co-authors of Weird Church*

"Great worship re-connects us with all of life. Yet so many of our churches are profoundly disconnected from the communities right at their doorstep. *Building Worship Bridges* leaves no stone, no truss, no process unturned as it expertly re-attaches worship to mission. Whether your church is 50 members or 5000, this practical guidebook will help your church rebuild the spiritual bridge into your neighbors' lives."

**Sally Morgenthaler,** *author, Worship Evangelism*

"*Building Worship Bridges* helps transform worship into a missional experience on behalf of members, new people, and the community. Every page is filled with ideas and insights that you can adapt to move from being a '*Decelerating Church*' to an '*Accelerating Church*.'"

**Lovett H. Weems, Jr.**
*Distinguished Professor of Church Leadership at Wesley Theological Seminary*

"This resource deploys the user-friendly metaphor of a bridge to help any church examine and enhance the 'nuts and bolts' of creating relevant worship to reach its community. Thanks to Cathy, Kay and Bob for creating what has the potential to help many congregations move forward."

**Rev. Sue Nilson Kibbey,** *Director Office of Missional Church Development of the West Ohio Conference of The United Methodist Church*

# Endorsements

"Participating in and then coaching churches that have reached new people in their respective communities, Bob, Cathy, and Kay write from personal experiences of both success and failure; and readers are the better for it. If you're looking for a "user-friendly" guide to constructing relevant worship experiences that build bridges to the community, this book is for you."

**Jim and Kim Griffith,** *Griffith Coaching*

"Fixing worship is about a lot more than getting a projector or a bass player. *Building Worship Bridges* has a rich mix of adaptive and technical insights into how you can open your church up to the winds of spirit and inspiration that are the foundation of authentic worship. If you're struggling to find and share the joy, comfort and refreshment of divine worship, *Building Worship Bridges* is what you're looking for."

**Rev. Stephan Ross,** *Vital Church Project Director, Oregon-Idaho*

"When I picked up *Building Worship Bridges*, I found a valuable resource. Explaining that worship must connect with new people as well as regular attenders, the authors present five phases to make the worship journey fruitful. As the book follows a worshiper who has different worship experiences at two churches, it reveals areas of worship needing improvement and provides practical fixes. Timely and well-presented, *Building Worship Bridges* is a "must read" for pastors, church leaders, and worship teams."

**Dirk Elliott,** *Director of New Church Development, Michigan Area*

"One of the dirty little secrets in churches is that people won't invite other people because the worship is boring. This book helps churches confront and change that reality. With practical advice and concrete steps, the resources here will immediately help teams rethink what they do week in and week out."

**Matt Miofsky,** *Lead Pastor of The Gathering, St. Louis, MO*

# Endorsements _____

"At the heart of what it means to be a disciple of Jesus Christ is the call to worship. While this calling is bigger than a worship service, the worship service is very often the entry point into a lifestyle of worship. *Building Worship Bridges* encourages us to do the worship service well so that people have every opportunity to encounter the loving presence of God. It even gives the tools to help make that happen. A great resource for all who know that great worship can lead to great discipleship and great kingdom impact."

**Dr. Phil Maynard,** *author, coach, and speaker*

"If you are a preacher or worship leader this book will be perfect for you and your team. *"Building Worship Bridges"* is more than a metaphor—it is a mandate to create worship that connects with your community mission field. In it (and in its accompanying workbook) you'll learn to start with the spiritual 'why' and then how to do the right things in the right way for the right reasons to accelerate your church's growth."

**Jim Ozier,** *New Church Development & Congregational Transformation of the North Texas Conference of The United Methodist Church*

"At last a book that provides the building blocks for compelling worship! Thank you, Cathy Townley, Kay Kotan, and Bishop Robert Farr for this excellent resource! *Building Worship Bridges* will help worship teams from local churches connect to their larger communities. These teams will be guided on how to create worship that reaches new people, younger people and more diverse people. A great r esource for new church plants and existing congregations."

**Rev. Dr. Douglas Ruffle,** *Associate Executive Director, Path 1*

"In this day and age, one can spend seemingly unlimited resources trying to develop a church that can cross contextual divides and connect a city with the living Christ through meaningful, relevant, inspiring worship. Cathy Townley, Kay Kotan and Bishop Robert Farr have succeeded in creating a worship resource that can save time, money, and tears. Adaptable and life giving, this book is a must read for church leaders trying to take things to the next level."

**Eric Bjorklund,** *Worship Pastor*
*Centennial UMC, St. Anthony Park Campus, St. Paul, MN*

## Kissing Your Fear of Bridges on the Nose ...

Do you have gephyrophobia? That is the fear of crossing bridges. Yes, the fear of crossing bridges is a "thing." If you have that fear, you may already know what we are talking about since you are getting ready to cross a bridge as you read this book. We are asking you to cross a worship bridge.

The panic attack is brewing. Perhaps you have already broken into a sweat. You are light headed and dizzy. Your heart is racing. Those symptoms cause you to close your eyes as you cross the worship bridge. We are asking you to keep your eyes open. The sight will be beautiful and we do not want you to miss it. Your church's missional focus could be your miracle cure for your fear of bridges.

We will remove obstacles and encourage abundant two-way traffic across the worship bridge, coming and going between your church and the community. Then you will see more and more new people come into a relationship with Christ and with the Christian Church. Yes, keep your eyes open. It is time to kiss your gephyrophobia on the nose. Just put one foot in front of the next as you take your first step upon the worship bridge.

# Foreword _____

During my forty years of ministry, I have been blessed to consult with hundreds of congregations and visit or preach in hundreds more. The focus of my ministry, through a variety of different roles, has always been to increase the number of vital congregations that have the capacity to change individual lives, communities and the world. I have observed and learned much. One of the most significant truths about congregational vitality is this: the worship service is either the accelerant or decelerant for a church's mission and disciple-making. The worship service leads to numerous opportunities to build bridges between the church and the neighborhood, or it causes a disconnect.

*Building Worship Bridges* nails this truth. Cathy Townley, Kay Kotan and Bishop Farr have written a compelling and helpful volume that lifts up the centrality of the worship service to congregational vitality and provides specific insights and tools to create a culture of worship excellence and missional impact.

Alan Hirsch, the Australian missiologist and author of numerous books, including *The Forgotten Way: Reactivating the Missional Church,* claims that worship is about becoming like Jesus. The central premise in much of his teaching is that we are all being profoundly discipled by the culture and that consumerism is the alternative religion of our day. The culture is shaping our sense of meaning, purpose, identity and belonging. In this sense, everyone is a disciple of something or someone, and no one can avoid being discipled.

Christian worship is the principal antidote to being discipled by the culture. Authentic, compelling, high-quality worship is counter-cultural because it focuses our attention on God's purposes, not our consumer-prone preferences. Such worship shapes our identity as a child of God, brings meaning to our lives and addresses our desire to belong to one another and a greater purpose. As Townley, Kotan and Farr state so clearly, "Worship is mission. It's a journey with a destination: to find ourselves in God."

In my experience, congregations that are *Building Worship Bridges* to "accelerate the traffic flow" between the church and the mission field are first and foremost devoted to Christ's missional imperatives to grow in love of God and neighbor, reach new people and heal a broken world. Their worship planning is driven by devotion to the mission (to make disciples of Jesus Christ for the transformation of the world). All design elements of their worship compel us to respond to God's love and embrace Christ's mission.

As I read the *Building Worship Bridges* manuscript, the Acts 2 description of the early church's worship kept coming to mind.

*That day about three thousand took him at his word, were baptized and were signed up. They committed themselves to the teaching of the apostles, the life together, the common meal, and the prayers.*

*Everyone around was in awe—all those wonders and signs done through the apostles! And all the believers lived in a wonderful harmony, holding everything in common. They sold whatever they owned and pooled their resources so that each person's need was met.*

*They followed a daily discipline of worship in the Temple followed by meals at home, every meal a celebration, exuberant and joyful, as they praised God. People in general liked what they saw. Every day their number grew as God added those who were saved.*

**Act 2:42-47 (MSG)**

It is clear the church has always excelled and accelerated in its mission through its worship of the Lord of the Church. The world has changed dramatically and at an increasingly relentless pace since those post-Pentecost days of the early church. This is evident in the acknowledgment of current reality and contemporary best practices throughout *Building Worship Bridges*. But, what has not changed from the birth of the church is the centrality of worship to form disciples that can transform the world. Worship itself is the bridge that allows disciples of Christ to make new disciples of Jesus Christ for the transformation of the world.

Thank you, Cathy, Kay and Bishop Farr, for calling us back to this truth, while offering immensely practical steps to *Building Worship Bridges*. This book will become a valued resource for any local church worship team that desires their worship to add energy and focus to the congregation's mission of attracting, forming and equipping disciples of Jesus. I celebrate all the congregations all over North America that will accelerate their missional impact because they engage these pages.

**Bishop Bruce R. Ough**
Dakotas-Minnesota Area
The United Methodist Church

# Part One

# Bridging the Worship Gap

# Introduction _____

## Intentionality

Our intention in providing this resource is to offer not only solutions, but also hope to pastors, leaders and congregations. Some who pick up this resource do so knowing their current reality while others might still be in denial. Our experience would indicate that most churches know they are struggling with reaching new people, but have run out of ideas on how to "fix it."

Even for those that know they need to change, we have found that most do not attribute the disconnect between the church and the neighborhood to the worship service itself. Recognizing the disconnect and attributing that disconnect in large part to the collapse of the worship service "bridge" is critical to finding the fixes, even if it is all so hard to hear at times. Our bottom line motivating factor in this resource is to provide hope, healing, and strategies to reach more people for Jesus Christ. Faithful servant, don't despair, have hope with perseverance!

We also want to reach out specifically to smaller churches. We are aware some might think they do not have the ability to do the things we are suggesting, and that only larger sized corporate churches can grow and build worship bridges. Again, please be encouraged. Your church has the ability to build a bridge with the neighborhood regardless of your size.

We, the authors, have all spend a significant amount of our ministry time involved in both very large churches and small churches as leaders and staff. We also all coach larger and much smaller churches. Small churches can learn a lot from larger churches. We are excited to help churches of any size discover their potential for accelerating neighborhood connections through worship.

**CT-KK-BRF**

## Run Your Race...

[12-14] *I'm not saying that I have this all together, that I have it made. But I am well on my way, reaching out for Christ, who has so wondrously reached out for me. Friends, don't get me wrong: By no means do I count myself an expert in all of this, but I've got my eye on the goal, where God is beckoning us onward—to Jesus. I'm off and running, and I'm not turning back.*

**Philippians 3:12-14 MSG**

# Chapter One

## Disastrous Bridge Collapses

*The I-35W Mississippi River bridge was an eight-lane, steel truss arch bridge that carried Interstate 35W across the Saint Anthony Falls of the Mississippi River in Minneapolis, Minnesota. During the evening rush hour on August 1, 2007, it suddenly collapsed, killing 13 people and injuring 145.[1]*

Cathy, a resident of the Minneapolis - St. Paul Twin City area, remembers that night in vivid detail. It was a Wednesday night. She was in the midst of leading a worship service when one of the pastors interrupted the music to make the announcement about the disastrous bridge collapse and lead the congregation in prayer.

Cathy's prayers went up fervently to God. Her young adult kids were commuters to and from school and work and were often on that bridge during evening rush hour. She was so grateful to find out later they were okay – one of them having driven off the bridge a mere ten minutes before tragedy struck. Cathy and her husband were intensely relieved and simultaneously heartbroken for those whose lives changed that night.

In the hours, days and months following the I-35W bridge collapse, engineers and city planners determined that the bridge collapsed because the bridge's gusset plates failed.[2] That set off a firestorm of research among engineers and city planners worldwide to determine if their steel truss arch bridges' gusset plates were viable and could structurally support the traffic using the bridge. While there have been other disastrous bridge collapses

---

[1] https://en.wikipedia.org/wiki/I-35W_Mississippi_River_bridge
[2] Gusset plates are "thick sheets of steel that are used to connect beams and girders to columns or to connect truss members."

around the world in the 21st Century before and after the I-35W tragedy, none exposed the lack of attention to infrastructure like that one did.

Nine years later (as we write this book), Cathy has not forgotten the feeling of panic that set in as she worried about her own kids' fate that night. She was repeatedly reminded how close it came for at least a few years after the collapse because there were so many Twin Cities residents who were directly impacted by what happened. It was hard not to talk about it with people you kept running into.

Then there is the worship connection. Cathy, a worship start-up and worship transformation coach and consultant, has often thought of the I-35W Bridge collapse as a metaphor for the declining worship attendance in the mainline church in America.

## A Worship-bridge metaphor

The worship service has the potential and the responsibility to be a bridge that connects your church to your neighborhood. The bridge helps new Christ followers, formerly churched persons[3] and seeking unbelievers worship Christ through the Christian church alongside church regulars. A bridge connects two bodies of land to each other over a gap that has separated the land (like a river valley). The same is true for a worship bridge.

The worship bridge connects two bodies over a gap. A worship bridge connects the church to the neighborhood to help the church provide worship experiences for newer, more diverse populations. The church and the neighborhood are naturally separated by the countercultural nature of the church (the gap).

---

[3] Cathy attended a seminar in 2015 led by researcher Ed Stetzer, who said that the majority of new people we'll reach are dechurched more than truly unchurched. Here also is a post by Stetzer's coworker, Phil Nation, regarding who it is we are actually reaching when we reach new people: http://www.christianitytoday.com/edstetzer/2010/august/back-to-church-sunday-reaching-unchurched-and-dechurched.html

The church needs bridges to connect churched and unchurched populations by sharing the message of Jesus Christ to new people in a way new people understand.

To be a bridge, the worship service must be designed appropriately. Designing a worship service as a two-way bridge to and from the community is what this book and its companion workbook are about! We will not elaborate here on specific worship design content, except to say that solid construction will help a worship service endure and even increase in size in the same way physical bridge construction supports traffic flow. In many churches, the worship bridge is not enduring because the worship design elements the church uses work against the church's ability to speak to new people in a new way. When the worship service is not a bridge, it is the opposite. Instead, it is a disconnect. A service that is so "not engaging" for new people widens the gap between the church and the neighborhood.

*The service that is not a bridge is like the collapsed I-35W bridge of 2007. With a collapsed worship bridge, worship does not provide people to flow in and out of the church narrowing the gap between the churched and unchurched.*

The Mississippi River cuts through the heart of Minneapolis (technically dividing Minneapolis and St. Paul, Minnesota). Steel-truss arch bridge construction formed the road that was the interstate across the Mississippi River. Worship bridges are the road across the natural, countercultural gap that surrounds the church. A worship bridge provides two-way traffic. One direction is people coming into worship and being transformed. The other direction is people experiencing worship and being transformed only to bring others back with them to the worship service. People may also find themselves to be led across the worship bridge due to a connection with an outwardly focused event where personal connections are made with the churched people. What happens between worship services, the worship journey, is the transformational piece that bridges the gap of churched and unchurched.

## Building Worship Bridges: The Fundamentals

When you consider the bridge construction of a steel truss arch bridge (like the collapsed I-35W bridge) and apply that construction to the worship bridge, you will discover why some worship services are not bridges, and in fact, are a disconnect. [4]While each step and element of a bridge are key, we call your attention to six fundamentals of bridge building. Those fundamentals are the footings, the piers, the trusses, the gusset plates, the floor beams and the roadway. Please keep in mind this metaphor is a means of helping you, the reader, more easily capture the understanding of creating a worship experience to reach new people. We do not claim to be engineers and ask for apologies and grace upfront for any elements that might not pass the engineering or scientific minds' scrutiny. Please see this as a teaching tool for those desiring to create more effective worship that reaches new people rather than anything scientific.

---

[4] We apologize to our engineer friends for any oversimplification you may perceive in our use of steel-truss-arch bridge construction to describe how worship is a bridge!

## Worship Bridge Design Sketch[5]

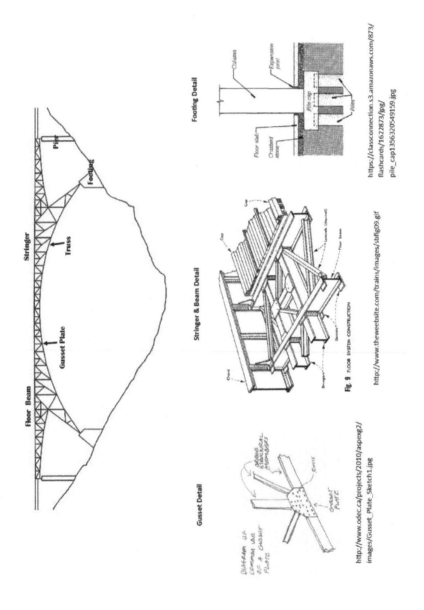

[5] http://www.highestbridges.com/wiki/images/thumb/1/1f/NewRiverArchTruss1725.
jpg/750px-NewRiverArchTruss1725.jpg

## The Six Fundamentals

**The Footings = Missional Focus.** The footings are placed deep below ground level on native, undisturbed soil to provide solid support for the structure. Footings can be of various materials, but are often concrete and reinforced with rebar. In *Building Worship Bridges*, the footing is the mission of making disciples. Making disciples is the very foundation in which the church exists. Without proper footings, any bridge will collapse. The same is true with a worship bridge. Without the "footings" of the missional focus of growing in our own faith and reaching new people to faith, we will collapse as a church. In our *Building Worship Bridges* metaphor, we will refer to "missional focus" as the terminology of the footings. The goal of the worship service is to increase the numbers of disciples of Jesus Christ that gather to praise God together. Bridge-like worship inspires discipleship for new persons and church regulars. A missional focus leads to creating an invitational culture for worship.

**The Piers = Discipleship.** The piers are classically concrete columns poured on top of the footings and reinforced with rebar for further stability. Piers are typically placed deep below the surface and continue above the surface. Just like footings, piers are foundational to holding the bridge up and supporting the infrastructure of the roadway. In terms of building a worship bridge, the all-important piers represent discipleship. If the footings are clearly understood as the purpose of the church as making disciples, the piers represent the intentional process for doing so. In other words, it is an intentional faith development process.

**The Trusses = Worship Elements.** Trusses describe the structure or formation of connecting elements. Trusses are normally large pieces of steel attached together to form the infrastructure that supports the bridge and ultimately the road to bridge the gap for travel. These are sometimes collectively referred to as beams, posts, rafters and struts. The intersection of these materials can form a rectangle, square or triangle. Most often, trusses come together in a triangular fashion offering the strongest and most durable connection. In looking at a bridge, this is usually the most obvious visual part of the bridge. For a worship bridge, the trusses represent all the various and important worship elements. These include such elements as technology, artistry, hospitality (including acts of welcoming, kids' ministries and music), worship access, worship visibility, and worship impact.

**The Gusset Plates = Missional Worship.** A steel truss arch bridge has gusset plates for stability for its steel trusses which provide the support for the needed road. Many gusset plates are shaped in triangles to allow for maximum support and durability. The gusset plates connect and stabilize the trusses. Engineers theorized that the gusset plates of the I-35W Bridge were too small to support the traffic on a busy interstate. One side or perhaps multiple sides of the gusset plates had corroded. Metaphorically, the gusset plates for *Building Worship Bridges* are a missionally-focused worship service. Having worship that is based in knowing the purpose of the church is to make disciples and practices doing so with intentionality. Keep in mind, the size of the worship gusset plate needs to be large enough to stabilize the worship bridge. In other words, our missional focus in worship must be size appropriate to provide the stability needed for today and the days to come.

**Floor Beams = Quality and Transformation.** In bridge construction, there are floor beams with perpendicular stringers that lay on top of the trusses. The floor beams and their adjoining stringers are the foundation for the road bed. Without floors beams and stringers, there would be no method of laying the road bed. This is yet another critical phase of bridge construction. While the trusses are often the most visible part of the bridge, the floor beams provide the very purpose of the bridge – to provide the road. The floor beams and stringers are the icing on the structural cake. For worship bridges, the floor beams are quality and the stringers are transformation. The beams and stringers refer to the quality of seeking excellence in the worship experience and the willingness for continual transformation. The value of continual transformation is both in the worship service itself and the leaders of worship. We must be continually adapting, improving, and seeking the most effective methods in deepening the faith of those in worship and bringing new people to faith. Newer, younger, more diverse persons will not stick at a worship service that is poor quality. They perceive poor quality worship as the church's lack of caring about them and God.

The quality value is an aspect of the authenticity of the church in creating enduring worship services. If we authentically care about fulfilling our missional focus, we will strive to make the service excellent. The mission field is always changing. Enduring worship services therefore also always change (methodologies) to continue to communicate with newer, younger, more diverse populations. Change shows up in worship services through cultural relevance. Discipled worshippers accept cultural relevance because they care more about fulfilling their calling to make new disciples than they do about familiarity. We cannot excellently fulfill our mission without continual change.

**The Roadway = Worship Journey.** Once the bridge is built, the very last part of the project is to lay the road bed. The road bed is sometimes concrete and other times it is asphalt. Sometimes it is a combination of both. The roadway provides the intended outcome of the bridge – to close the gap between two different

[6] Cathy's book Missional Worship distinguishes between the 24x7 rela-tionship with God aspect of worship and the one-hour-per-week worship service. You need both to develop authentic worship experiences. Mis-sional Worship: Increasing Attendance and Expanding the Boundaries of the Church, © 2007, Chalice Press.

bodies of land. For our worship bridge, the roadway signifies the worship journey. The worship journey is the 24/7 resulting experience from the worship service. Worship is our 24/7 relationship with God. The roadway (aka worship journey) on our worship bridge provides two-way traffic coming to and going from the church. Physical bridges are always north and south or east and west. The worship bridge is also two-ways if your purpose is to make new disciples of Jesus Christ. A one-way bridge is a collapsed bridge. New people will rarely attend a church in which members stay inside that church all the time. They wouldn't know the church was there! Worship bridge construction implies that the relevant, competent and compelling worship service that acts as a bridge grows from the relationship between church regulars and their guests - the people they invite. The worship service is an hour a week; the worship journey is our relationship with God, 24/7.[6]

Discipled Christians of all levels of discipleship follow God on the worship journey into the mission field; and then discipled Christians and their guests return to the gathering place to be part of the one-hour worship service. After participating in competent, compelling worship services, new and experienced disciples head out of the church building and back into the mission field to make more new disciples of Jesus Christ. The worship road bears the load of the worship service (all that goes into developing and hosting weekly worship) and the load of the increasing traffic upon the worship bridge.

The six elements above are the fundamentals in building worship bridges. We will more deeply explore each fundamental in the upcoming chapters. When we adopt, implement, and continuously improve these fundamentals, we will have the best opportunity of building a competent, compelling worship experience. In many mainline churches, many of the fundamentals of worship bridges are missing from worship service design, ultimately predetermining bridge collapse.

## A lack of infrastructure in the Mainline Church

In churches with a failed worship bridge, members crossed the bridge at one time in their life but then they let the road collapse behind them. Members are now stuck inside the church and no new people can get in. There is no reason to build a bridge over a land gap if you do not desire to get from one side to the other and back again. There is no need to build a worship bridge to bridge the worship gap if you do not desire to make new disciples who make new disciples. We will illustrate two-way bridge construction in the five chapters of Part Two of *Building Worship Bridges*: Worship, Hospitality, Technology, Discipleship and Artistry.

We hear the words, "boring, irrelevant, lethargic," to describe services that are a disconnect for new people. The boring, irrelevant, lethargic worship service has exposed a lack of infrastructure in the way we design and develop worship in our churches. That is another way of saying that the church is unhealthy. Another way to think about it is that the worship bridge is not structurally sound. The church may not have a missional focus, an intentional process to develop disciples, nor an emphasis on quality, hospitality or transformation. There is nothing to sustain worship service development in the church. That is a disastrous bridge collapse indeed.

Bishops and middle judicatories are trying to change systems to move churches toward health. It has been and will remain a long and difficult battle in systems as large and layered as most of our tribes are. They (Bishops and middle judicatories) should not stop their efforts, but real change will need to arise and accelerate through the local church. It will be led by pastoral leaders that are personally and passionately devoted to mission and not the personal preferences of many of the members that do not even know the church needs a new bridge. Some leaders will lead congregations to build completely new bridges while others will redesign existing bridges. Either way, we will be *Building Worship Bridges* for as far into the future as we can see from local church to local church.  Building sound worship bridges is how the church will gain and/or remain competent and compelling throughout the generations, for old and new alike. We cannot stop *Building Worship Bridges.* Ever!  Sadly, so many of us have stopped building and redesigning worship bridges. Local churches must decide to make *Building Worship Bridges* their utmost priority and not depend on districts, conferences, bishops, district superintendents or other judicatory leaders to design or build bridges for them.

---

[7] In their book, Ten Prescriptions for a Healthy Church, authors Bob Farr and Kay Kotan say, "As worship goes, so goes everything else," p.27. Ten Prescriptions for a Healthy Church, (c) Bob Farr and Kay Ko-tan, Abingdon Press, 2015

# Chapter Two _____

## Grow Healthy Churches to
## Build Worship Bridges

The mainline church has been lamenting our decline for decades. What has been missing from those conversations is the worship factor. There are numerous seminars you can participate in and books you can purchase that help you learn to get out of your church and into your neighborhood. All of that is good. But until we fix the worship service problem, outreach efforts will still fail. Without a compelling and competent worship service to invite new people to, there is no real way for the church to grow.

We, the authors, have never been to a declining church in which we did not have to address the impact of the declining worship service upon the overall life of the church. We have never been to a growing church in which the worship service was . . . well, bad. How goes worship, so goes the rest of the church.[7]

We can change the worship service after we learn how to do outreach, or we can learn how to do outreach through *Building Worship Bridges*. Most outreach activities are not rocket science. We will give you some ideas about how to get out into your church's neighborhood, though outreach activities per se are not our focus. Get Their Name by Farr & Kotan is a great resource for evangelism as a companion read. *Building Worship Bridges* will help you do things that naturally enable connections with new people.

### The unhealth of churches

The desire to reach new people with our missional focus is

the key fundamental part of the life of the church. It is the footing of your worship bridge. Churches with a missional focus will do whatever it takes to create a worship service new people want to attend. A missional focus is a sign of good health. Churches $_\times$ without a missional focus are not healthy churches. Some might be offended at our suggestion that declining churches are not healthy (aka lacking or unstable footings). Denial? If the purpose of the churches' existence is to make disciples of Jesus Christ for the transformation of the world, it would stand to reason that if we are not making disciples we are not serving the purpose and therefore some unhealthiness is imminent.

Many blame the decline of the mainline church on 21st Century attendance patterns. In our experience, regular attendance in our present day translates to 1.5 to 2 times per month. Whereas in the past decades, regular attenders came to church at least three times per month. Yet churches that are currently growing report increased worship attendance overall even though their regulars attend less frequently, too. Changing worship patterns are no real excuse for lack of growth. It is the health of the church (with a missional focus) that most impacts the church's ability to grow and develop worship services that function as bridges.

Familiarity may be one of the leading causes of decline. In churches making decisions based on personal, insider preference (not mission), members and their leaders take great pains not to offend anyone. They act like dysfunctional families that hide problems overtly as they gossip behind the backs of siblings and cousins (church members). They fight over meaningless things like the color of carpeting. They elevate old-timers to matriarch and patriarch status and then the powerful old-timer controls decisions and stops change. The closed family system ethos prefers decline over healthy conversations about reaching new people.

Changing a worship service in a church that is stuck in inward preservation is the last thing that would happen. Services typically date back decades, maybe to the time that church started (1950, 1960, 1980, 2000). For a new person, attending this service would be like stepping off an airplane in a country in which he does not know the native tongue and there is no translator. The style is foreign. The language is insider. The physical environment is cluttered, dated and in need of repair.

There is not much for kids. The quality of the music is poor, regardless of musical genre. Sermons are esoteric and meandering instead of insightful about how God can change your life. The environment is "not normal" and you do not fit in. You are a foreigner in a foreign land!

When you do not fit into a church environment, you cannot learn about Jesus at that church. Spiritually growing members left a long time ago. If they were not soured by the unhealthy behavior of church members, they probably found their way to a missionally focused church. But if the church experience soured someone who wanted to grow spiritually, the familiarity focused church ethos may have led them to determine there was not any church that could be the place that could help them. The bridge collapsed with people on it. The behavior of an ingrown church is not innocuous; it is potentially harmful.

### The culture (and the counterculture paradox)

Compare the non-missional church to a church that is missional (a healthy, invitational church). The methods used in our secular culture to communicate with people are also used in worship services in missional churches. The methods people have become accustomed to in everyday life, are the same methods used to help them learn about Jesus. Churches sometimes get stuck in a particular method as being sacred (instead of the practice of praise being the sacred thing). For example, some declining churches may feel that the only method to use music to praise God is with an organ and hymn book. It is not the method of the organ that is sacred, it is praising God that is sacred. Therefore, a missionally focused church would research music that is culturally relevant so that new people could find Jesus in music that is appealing and relevant to them.

Let's examine some examples of how culture impacts worship for missionally focused churches. In a worship service that acts as a bridge, you will see videos to explore spiritual matters.[8]

Overt use of technology reveals more technology behind the scenes and people that know how to run it. The church has spent money to hire a tech director (if they can afford it), or instead trains a tech savvy volunteer to develop the ministry. The quality-bar is held high; volunteers strive to do well like paid staff would. Sermons are vernacular (using every day, non-intimidating language). Prayers are vernacular, too (not flowery but relatable for the average unchurched person).

The person looking for a church experience would likely attend this service (because of its reputation and invitational practices); he is likely to fit in. The environment is "normal" – like daily life – thus enabling new relationships: between the new person and God, the new person and the church, the new person and Christian community, and even the new person within him/herself. Discipleship is beginning right now, even if at the smallest level.

*Building Worship Bridges* is a cultural endeavor, which uncovers an uncomfortable paradox for the church. The church is set apart; we are countercultural. But we do not stay countercultural unless we stay connected to the culture. Think about it: talking about Jesus to new people (countercultural) must be vernacular (cultural) since none of us hear the truth about our own lives apart from our own lives (cultural) – not new and not old. The context of the culture that is recognizable to us facili-

---

[8] In an article by Lovett H. Weems, we see that attendance patterns for church growth have everything to do with the willingness of a congregation to change their worship services. Those that don't change decline. Most do not change what they do. This article is a must-read!! https://www.churchleadership.com/leading-ideas/changing-congregational-trends/

tates our hearing of countercultural truths. A church that learns to engage the culture in order to express countercultural truths is a healthy church because they are who they are all the time: Christ followers. Healthy churches engage the culture to be countercultural.

Many churches fear enculturation as a result of using the culture to design and lead public worship. That is a misguided worry. The true opposite of countercultural is not cultural; it is isolation! The church growing isolated from the neighborhood is a worry that should keep us up at night! Isolation is the end result of the inability to introduce cultural relevance into worship design. Isolation leads to the very thing that got us to this discussion in the first place: church decline.

### The Calling to ACCELERATE Bridge-Building

The boring, irrelevant, lethargic worship service has been part of the problem of decline for all the decades the mainline church has been discussing decline. We must redesign our worship bridges or build new worship bridges if we are to stop and reverse the decline. We must return to being a church with a missional focus. We must have a sense of urgency! The time is NOW to be *Building Worship Bridges*!

**There is no time to waste.** People are falling off worship bridges as the bridges are collapsing beneath them! Or, they are not getting on worship bridges at all because the bridge is non-existent! We must once again accept responsibility for the souls God has put before us in our local communities. *Building Worship Bridges* matters to the local church's growth and influence in their community and possibly also to their tribe.

**It is time to promote Jesus.** Our need for speed is not to save our tribes; it is to reclaim who we are as the church (which might save our tribes). We are "Christians." That means we follow Jesus. In our non-church-centric culture, we can find many compelling beliefs apart from Christianity, some of which seem helpful. Still, if you are a Christ follower, it would be, well, normal that you would think that Jesus is still more powerful than the competition. That does not mean any of us have license to thump Bibles on everyone's head.

Not even God coerces us to believe. Still, there should be some passion for the son of God in a way that makes the hope of the Gospel stand out to anyone who is paying attention. Alas, that is not what we, the authors, see. From local church to local church we find tepid expressions of Jesus, except in the churches that are growing, regardless of theological perspective. A growing progressive church may tell a different story about Jesus than a growing orthodox or conservative church; left or right does not seem to matter. Passion for Jesus matters! For the person that is looking for meaning through the local church, it is meaningless to be at a church that has a tepid expression of Jesus. If we are not convinced that Jesus changes lives, why would we bother to be the Christian church? Let's get a move on to be who we are: Christ followers.

**God has called us to this time.** Making worship changes most always produces pushback. A power boost to the faith community occurs when pushback does not cause a competent leader to sway from the purpose God has entrusted to her. Instead the competent leader holds firm to the mission to build worship bridges and make new disciples. Now the faith community has more energy for growth. Speed is important because it shows that the primary spiritual leader of the faith community has a burning desire to serve Christ. She cannot rest because the mission is driving her forward. That drive to be who we are (Christ followers) impacts growth overall.

Without that drive, we are at square one. We are not called to our positions as spiritual leaders to be at square one.

# Technical AND adaptive change
# bring health to the church

In Chapter One, we introduced the six fundamentals of bridge construction. For worship bridges, the floor beams are quality and the stringers are transformation. There are two very different types of stringers (transformation) that will be necessary in *Building Worship Bridges.* Those two stringers, or transformations are technical and adaptive change. Change, both technical and adaptive, is necessary to help improve church health to help you build a strong worship bridge.

Technical changes are what we apply to things that need fixing that we often know how to fix. *Building Worship Bridges* requires numerous technical changes, some of which may be easier to implement than we might think. For example, introducing new musical styles into existing worship is a technical change. We can learn how to play new music or we can identify someone who already knows how. All that is easy, until you add in the "willingness factor:" Are we willing to let new music into the service that we like just the way it is? Adaptive change is required for technical changes to take root. Churchgoers must adapt their thinking and behavior to accept and support the process of doing certain things in new ways. While technical change is often easier to implement than we think, adaptive change is often much harder. But you already knew that!

Adaptive change affects behavior and culture. When a congregation adapts to new ways of worship, they grow spiritually healthy and strong. *Healthy and strong disciples are reproducing disciples.* We notice unpaid laypersons taking the lead in influencing their peers toward spiritual growth in adaptive congregations. This happens because the layperson has personally adapted to technical changes and the congregation trusts them because they are peers that have grown spiritually. It is difficult for a church to raise up lay spiritual leaders without pastoral and any paid or unpaid staff that behave also as spiritual leaders. That means that the pastor and paid staff must also change adaptively. Adaptive change is a chain reaction. Adaptive change is sometimes a slow process that brings people along with the missional focus.

An example of adaptive change from a pastor or other staff as spiritual leaders is when the pastor or paid staff holds firm to the mission in the face of pushback against the mission. It might sting to say to the naysayer, "We are going to keep going with this new direction as a church even if you personally do not want to join us."

But it is exactly what a mature, pastoral or staff spiritual leader would say (nicely!). It will be tempting when hearing the naysayer's anger and frustration to not try to ameliorate their difficulty with change by saying, "Just kidding; we are not going to follow the mission Jesus gave us as the church."

It is hard to lose the very people you thought were with you once upon a time. The powerful tradeoff is that leading adaptively allows you to raise up more lay spiritual leaders and fulfill the very mission God calls the church to: making new disciples of Jesus Christ for the transformation of the world!

Everyone's adaptive change is important in the church. But the most important adaptive change of all is going to come from the pastoral leader. If the lead pastor does not change adaptively, and thus if he or she is unable to hold the line of mission, no other adaptive change will endure.

Sometimes we, the authors, work with church staffs and laypersons that want to see their local church environment change. If the pastor is not on board, it does not work. A non-missional pastor will too easily bond with non-missional laypersons. We call that a power block. It is a stale mate.

Pastors, you must lead this change! If you are to succeed, you will not lead the change alone; you will bring others along. But you must still be the leader. We will help you set up systems for technical worship changes throughout *Building Worship Bridges*. We will speak plainly to what it will take for you and your staff to lead these changes adaptively in a way that raises up more lay spiritual leaders. We have based much of our writing in *Building Worship Bridges* upon the interplay between technical and adaptive change for growing churches healthy enough to build new and enduring worship bridges. There are ten construction principles that are a combination of technical and adaptive change principles. We introduce them in Chapter Three. They form the skeleton of Part Two, and you will base bridge construction upon these ten construction principles.

# Chapter Three _____

## A Construction Manual

The primary goal of *Building Worship Bridges* is to help you develop compelling worship services that connect both regulars and new people to God and each other. Missionally focused churches understand that the priority is reaching new people.

The second goal of *Building Worship Bridges* is to increase the traffic flow of new people and regulars on your worship bridge with a certain level of momentum. We, the authors, would like to help you fulfill both the primary and secondary goals, using our experiences of building various worship bridges ourselves over the years.

### The writers and your construction partners in *Building Worship Bridges:*

**Cathy** has started worship services and churches and has served in numerous capacities in new church development, including worship. She serves as a coach for HCI (Healthy Church Initiative) and continues to serve as a church planting coach and worship consultant across the country.

Cathy teaches worship and church planting workshops. She has evaluated too many worship services to count in a variety of settings, from very small to very large in nearly every mainline denomination. Cathy also continues to work for her home Conference (the Minnesota Annual Conference and the Dakotas-Minnesota Episcopal Area of the United Methodist Church) in a coaching and consulting role for worship and new church development.

**Kay** is a professionally credentialed coach who has coached hundreds of pastors and churches across the nation helping them become more vital in reaching new people. She has authored more than a dozen books on church and leadership transformation. Kotan served on the HCI Executive Team and was the primary creator of the Small Church Initiative under the HCI process. Kay is now serving as the Congregational Development Director for the Susquehanna Conference in Pennsylvania.

**Bishop Farr** started a church as the planting pastor and has pastored five different congregations in five very different settings that saw significant growth and impact in the communities they served. He has spent over nine years supervising scores of new church plants in the Missouri Conference of the United Methodist Church.

He developed the Healthy Church Initiative (HCI) for church transformation. This ministry is used nationally in the United Methodist church. Bishop Farr is currently serving as Bishop of the Missouri Annual Conference of The United Methodist Church.

### The Construction of Part Two: FIVE PHASES OF *Building Worship Bridges*

Part One of this book introduced you to why there is a need to redesign or build new worship bridges. Part One also introduced you to the bridge metaphor. As you begin your journey into the Part Two of the book, you will find there are five chapters (or construction sequences) that are devoted to different phases of worship development.

In each chapter, you will find both a technical and an adaptive construction principle. By the end of the book, you will have ten total construction principles – five technical and five adaptive – to help you in *Building Worship Bridges* and accelerating your growth through compelling worship services.

## The Ten Construction Principles

1. Tell God's Story (technical)
2. Tell Your Story (adaptive)
3. Pay Attention to First Impressions (technical)
4. Pay Attention to Quality (adaptive)
5. Enliven the First Ten Minutes (technical)
6. Enliven Spiritual Practices (adaptive)
7. Strengthen the Ending (technical)
8. Strengthen Design Processes (adaptive)
9. Run Transitions (technical)
10. Run the Race (adaptive)

In each chapter, you will find an introductory story followed by a sequence of topics that we have listed below for you to see at a glance. Absorbing the chapter flow will allow you to easily identify the process for *Building Worship Bridges* and know how to navigate this construction manual. Each chapter is organized by these nine different topics in the order listed below:

- Biblical Theme
- Technical principle
- Preparing Your Church for Guests
- The Guest Experience
- Guest Experience Debrief
- Adaptive principle
- Preparing Yourself for Guests
- The Leader Experience
- Leader Experience Debrief

We want you to understand what we are aiming for in this sequence. Please spend some time with our annotated list below:

**Biblical themes.** We will introduce at least one Biblical theme in every chapter. We, the authors, are not academics; we are missionaries. We will discuss the Biblical themes from our perspective and invite you to translate into your own language and context. Biblical themes are part of your missional infrastructure.

**Technical construction principle.** As mentioned above, you will find a principle that leads to technical change at the beginning of each chapter.

**Preparing Your Church for Guests.** This section helps you break down the Biblical themes (countercultural) into a cultural framework. Teach your congregation about cultural trends to lay the foundation for adaptive change.

**The Guest Experience.** You will follow a story line in this section from chapter to chapter about a guest who experiences worship at both Accelerating and *Decelerating Churches*, looking for a substantial encounter of God. You will get to consider the possible reactions of such a person that might show up at your church. The guest experience appears within the section on technical change because guests respond initially to the packaging of what you do. Nonetheless, the guest will quickly detect an inauthentic offering on the part of the church. If you are not seriously working on helping guests encounter Jesus, your guest will know it and will not stick around.

**Guest Experience Debrief.** We will pick apart the Guest Experience story to point out what was most helpful and most distracting for the guest to make a connection, and why. We will give you "a fix" to address unhelpful practices and embrace new and even best practices. We will elaborate upon various "fixes" in the workbooks that accompany *Building Worship Bridges*. The workbook will provide techniques and processes for you to adopt and adapt to your context.

**Adaptive Construction Principle.** As mentioned above, you will find a principle that leads to adaptive change at the beginning of this section. It will invite you to go deep within yourself and the culture of your church to create momentum in *Building Worship Bridges.*

**Preparing Yourself for Guests.** Regardless of your leadership role – whether in front of the congregation or behind the scenes – worship leadership is not entirely about performance. It is also about being transparent as you share your faith journey so that others can see what it means to be an ever-growing disciple of Jesus Christ. The role of any worship leader is to usher others into the presence of Christ. We must do so authentically, out of our own journey.

**The Leader Experience.** From chapter to chapter, you will follow the journey of a worship leader who moves through his own struggles toward authentic, up front spiritual leadership. *The Leader Experience* is as important as *The Guest Experience* and should dovetail at some point. Who is the leader and what does he or she do? See the heading, below: Construction workers needed.

**Leader Experience Debrief.** We will break down the leader story to think through why the leader is behaving in the way we are describing. As with the *Guest Experience,* we will give you "a fix" to address unhelpful practices and embrace new and even best practices for leading adaptive change. It is not just persons in seats that must change adaptively!

# Building Worship Bridges
*The Complete Construction Manual for Building Worship Bridges*

The Workbook is your *Complete Construction Manual for Building Worship Bridges.* Just like the book, the workbook corresponds to Part One and Part Two of the *Building Worship Bridges* book.

- Part One of the workbook, *"Bridging the Worship Gap,"* is a study guide for Part One of this book. Part One of the workbook corresponds to Chapters One through Four in *Building Worship Bridges*, the book.

- Part Two of the workbook, *"Five Phases of Building Worship Bridges,"* is a study guide and charts for Part Two of the book *Building Worship Bridges.* Part Two of the workbook corresponds to Chapters Five through Nine in the book.

The focus of the workbook, *Complete Construction Manual for Building Bridges,* is intensely practical to help you implement the ideas you are reading about in the book, *Building Worship Bridges.*

## Construction Workers Needed

No one person should go through this book or *Building Worship Bridges* alone. We suggest you have a team to work through the material together. Any time there is bridge construction, there are many workers sharing the work to complete the project. Reconstruction of the I-35W Bridge led to a population increase for a season in the Twin Cities as numerous construction workers moved there for many months. *Building Worship Bridges* requires many workers, too. Below you will find some helpful hints for gathering your worship bridge construction team:

**Worship leaders of all stripes**. Official roles include: pastors, choir directors, organists, song leaders, band leaders, liturgists, poets, artists, writers, dancers, various musicians and singers, various tech team people, the worship committee, the worship design team (if you have one) and the sermon writing team (if you have one). Additionally, you may wish to include persons who have a vested interest in seeing the worship service in your church improve. These persons are likely prominent influencers and decision makers perhaps on boards or councils.

**Worship teams**. Some churches have worship teams comprised of bands, singers, behind the scenes worship planners and other up front worship leaders. If you use the terminology "worship team," then whoever comprises that group in your church should work their way through *Building Worship Bridges* together. Additionally, include other "worship leaders of all stripes" with you.

**Younger (unchurched) leaders.** We, the authors, work with numerous millennials in our coaching and consulting. While many churches desire and have a mission field full of millennials, sometimes the millennials within our churches have limited insight and experience into reaching unchurched millennials. Younger leaders are important, but please do not overlook the true need for those who have been recently unchurched whom you are growing into disciples who can help you reach out to the unchurched population - regardless of age. We have found that even those with the strongest ability to interact with current culture often have very dated views of the worship service because they grew up in churches that had services that never left 1950. Part of our goal is to help very churched millennials learn how to communicate with the unchurched population of their own generation.

**Smaller to larger churches.** If your church is under 50 in worship, over 750 in worship, or somewhere in between those two numbers, it is likely you will need the material and suggestions in *Building Worship Bridges*. Even very large churches of over 1000 in worship can lose their way on reaching new people through their worship services. It is amazing to see how many very large churches start new services that do not make it. This material can help you utilize your massive resources to have an even greater impact in your location.

**Existing churches and new church starts.** The development of worship is going to be very similar regardless of if you are starting a new service, a new church, or if you are trying to transform an existing service. What may be different is the sequence and the adaptive change.

### Bridge-building Tools

Every construction worker, carpenter and bridge builder has tools they use to do their work. Likewise, we have provided learning tools to help you accelerate growth through compelling worship services. While some tools are generic tools used for a variety of projects, some tools have specialty uses. Bridge-building tools are no different. Here is a list of tools your worship bridge-builders will need in their toolbox:

**The construction principles.** These theories are based on the authors' experiences and best practices of principles used to develop powerful worship services that build bridges between the church and the secular culture. The construction principles will be introduced throughout the book, but you will find a completed listing of the principles at the end of this book for a quick reference.

**The charts.** There are numerous charts that will appear in the companion workbook. They are the most practical, visual tools in assisting you with constructing your worship bridge.

**The workbook.** We have already provided insight into the workbook in terms of style and function.

**Accelerating and** *Decelerating Churches.* Bridge-building churches accelerate growth – that is, they have increased traffic on the road across their worship bridge. Categorically we could call them *Accelerating Church.* Isolated churches do the opposite – that is, they have decreased traffic or the bridge has failed completely and no one can get on in either direction. Categorically we could call them *Decelerating Church.* We provide a chart comparing *Accelerating and Decelerating Churches* in our workbook, THE WORKBOOK: *Building Worship Bridges, The Complete Construction Manual for Building Worship Bridges.*

### Terminology and concepts

Starting a new service or a new church is a transformational process that requires new language and possible new definitions. Using this new language can help you move your bridge-building process forward. New terminology in the coming pages includes:

**Attraction (versus invitation or relationship).** You could try to build your worship bridge by attraction – that is, you build it so that they will come. However, if you ignore the relationship component, *Building Worship Bridges* will not work. As we have already said, powerful worship grows from your rela-

45

tionship with your mission field. It not the same thing to stare at your computer thinking up a worship service to go with the demographic study you read. That said, there is an attractional element of all worship service development that we cannot ignore.

The service must be well done with attention to detail and quality; it must be relevant to the mission field. Relevance causes the mission field to talk about the church experience amongst themselves – between the new people and their friends. Relationship development is at the center of this work, and relationships always lead to an attractional component. People attend churches they have heard about through their friends. We have taken the time to define the connection between attraction and relationships because there is a rumor afoot that says attraction is dead when it comes to *Building Worship Bridges*. Attraction is not dead. But it is not stand alone either.

**Called and gifted for worship leadership.** We are not appointing warm bodies to perform a role. That is a superficial approach to worship development. Many people are called to worship leadership in a variety of capacities. Being called is the key. This is a matter of the heart more than it is a matter of availability and sometimes even ability. Ability without heart is simply not going to work. New people will not connect to a skilled musician who does not have a heart for Jesus. New people desire to experience transparent, authentic leaders in worship who also have a good voice and can play a lead instrument.

**Compelling Worship.** Worship that engages persons in seats and never bores them is compelling. It is current and relevant to their lives. It is transformational, and propels worshippers back into their own lives where they interact with the mission field in a brand-new way. Their transformation led them there. Compelling worship makes disciples. Compelling worship creates a

24/7 worship journey (relationship with God). Think, "the most engaging movie of our time that elevates the outcome of good over evil." That's compelling. That's what the church should be expressing during every worship service. The compelling nature of Christianity leads to a compelling experience that transforms persons in seats to the point that they must share it with others.

**The guest (not the visitor).** A visitor is someone who drops by unannounced for whom we have made no special preparations. You might still be in your bathrobe when they show up! A guest is someone we have invited, made special preparations for and are looking forward to receiving. Guests recognize the savory smells of their favorite meatloaf wafting through the house as they enter. Use guest language to teach church regulars of any level (those that have been there a long time and those that are becoming regulars) that reaching new people in the church is about creating an invitational culture. A culture of invitation and expectation is key to anticipating guests each and every week rather than being okay with a visitor dropping by. This culture shift will change the way you do ministry!

**The Mission Field.** Some might call this your "target." The mission field is a group or groups of people that live in your church's neighborhood that may or may not know the God you worship (Jesus) and who don't have a relationship with your church or probably any church. Some do not like the language "mission field" because they feel it makes the church seem superior; like we have all the answers. Others choose "your neighborhood" or "your surrounding community." Find the language that is appropriate for your context. We will use the language *mission field* to describe your target group in your neighborhood and your surrounding community. Some might be reluctant to identify their mission field because it might seem limiting. Without identifying who God is calling us to reach specifically, we try to be all things to all people. When we do this, we dilute our ability to reach the target and therefore normally have a difficult time reaching anyone.

**Opting in (opt-in).** Worship designers and planners do not exist to force guests into making a connection with our church. Guests can choose on their own (opt-in) and we must let them. We trust their own ability to connect, with God's help. It is the work of the Holy Spirit. We practice due diligence in our work of worship planning and *Building Worship Bridges* to remove as many obstacles as we can that might provide a meaningful and authentic experience with God. We leave the end result to God and pray.

**Old and New.** We are referring to "new" seekers of Christianity to whom we reach out to make "new" disciples of Christianity. We refer to the already convinced as "old" disciples. We are not referring to age or even to longevity of the Christian experience with the word "old."

**Public Worship.** Public worship can be described as the public worship event, the worship service, the gathered community, and persons in seats. The worship service is not private. It is public. It does not matter where it is held. Even if you host the worship service in your church building, it is public. The worship service exists for those in the church and those not yet there because God loves both old and new (see above). We will refer to the worship service and those that attend it using the various terms above.

**Worship arts.** In our current culture, the wide range of music and other numerous artistic expressions in worship including technology are collectively considered The Worship Arts. This might include drama, liturgical dance, sound, lights, music, videos, chancel area décor, vocals, etc.

*[19]Speak to each other with psalms, hymns, and spiritual songs; sing and make music to the Lord in your hearts.*

**Ephesians 5:19,** CEB

In the ancient church, both before and during Jesus' time, we brought every part of our lives and creativity to the worship service. The resources may have been more limited, but the concept was for giving our all. In our current culture, giving our all means to include all areas of art and creative expression to communicate the meaning of the gospel in your context. No holding back! Look for specific examples in the companion workbook.

**Worship design team** *(not the Altar Guild or worship committee).* Historically, the Altar Guild had a primary focus on dressing the altar for the liturgical season and for communion Sunday. The design of the decor was often liturgical and formulaic with the same paraments from church to church, depending on the liturgical season. The Altar Guild morphed into the worship committee in many churches. Even in our current culture in *Decelerating Church*, the worship committee often continues to work apart from the sermon theme and again follows the liturgical season for décor. The worship committee also often critiques the service but does not implement any suggestions. Critiques often are about the service not meeting the personal needs of the committee and their friends - not missional alignment.

In our current culture, a worship design team is a creative team that collaboratively works with the pastor to invent a competent, compelling, culturally relevant bridge-building worship experience each and every time the worship service convenes. A worship design team is more expansive. By expansive we mean a variety of skills, gifts and callings to different aspects of the worship arts ministry area. It is more collaborative than either an Altar Guild or a worship committee. The design team is likely to decorate not only the altar but the entire worship space and perhaps even the entire building to suit the theme of the sermon and/ or to create the ambiance that will help the mission field fit in. The high functioning, missional worship design team is very self-critical because mission is the highest value and this team is devoted to making worship an environment in which old and new can experience God together.

**Worship in spirit and truth.** We are using this phrase throughout this book to indicate the passion that accompanies heart-felt worship. We invite your team to contextualize this phrase for your church in your own way.

**Worship style terminology.** We have not yet introduced language like "band led worship," "choir led worship," "spoken liturgy worship," and "ancient future worship." We feel it is better to introduce those terms in context. Look for them in your reading soon! Note that we down-play the language "contemporary" and "traditional" to describe worship. We will use "contemporary worship" and "traditional worship" language here and there in the pages to come, but it is very often misleading for church and unchurched persons. Ten different church people would give you ten different definitions of contemporary and traditional as those terms pertain to worship. If churched persons find those terms confusing, unchurched persons will find them a conundrum! If you can refer to the style of worship your church offers more descriptively (choir led, band led, etc.), new people might understand what you are talking about! Believe it or not, so will church people.

**Terminology reminder.** We have already introduced some new worship language such as "the upfront worship leader" and "the behind the scenes worship planner." Use these terms to deepen the worship ethos in your church and build a strong infrastructure for a compelling worship bridge.

# Chapter Four  _____

## Completing Construction

To complete and expedite *Building Worship Bridges*, we need construction deadlines. There is only so much money and so much time. Create your timeline and try to stick to the goals with minor adjustments and course corrections as needed. We will provide discussion opportunities in the workbook for you to discover your own ideal timeline for transforming existing bridges or building a brand-new bridge in your context.

Bridges by and large are beautiful and memorable structures all over the world. Some are quite famous and identifiable by the architectural art that has gone into their design and construction. Some bridges you only need to see a picture and you know which bridge it is and where it's located; the bridge is simply that well-known. The new I-35W Bridge is identifiable in this way. It features night lighting that sets it apart from other bridge structures in the Minneapolis-St. Paul area and from its previous design.

Some worship bridges are like that, too. Some churches have such well-known worship styles and services that we only need name the church and we can tell you what the worship service is like. For any growing church, the worship bridge is the thing that most identifies you to your neighborhood. When someone new is looking for a church, they will come to your church because of the visibility and perhaps familiarity your worship bridge has given you.

More importantly, if your worship bridge becomes visible, it will belie the deeper truth, that this is a church that is giving away Jesus. That is what new people are looking for or they would not be seeking a church. The unchurched may not use terminology quite like this, but they are looking for hope, peace, and something bigger than life. Giving away Jesus is the essence of *Building Worship Bridges*. And that is the bridge we want to help you build.

 **Let the work begin! Turn to the companion workbook, The** *Complete Construction Manual for Building Worship Bridges*, **online to get started.**

# Part Two

# Five Phases
# of Building
# Worship Bridges

# Chapter Five _____

## Phase One: Worship

In 1987 Cathy became a worship leader. She had no training for the job. But the church she was attending had decided to start a new service and Cathy had a background in music and theater, so she was asked to lead it. Cathy agreed. Her excitement wasn't about God as much as it was about the start-up process. At the time, Cathy didn't know she is what you would call a "church start-up person." She has learned the terminology since that time. But it was her natural gifting, as evidenced by the amount of startup work she had done in the arts throughout her life. Cathy enjoyed the limelight!

The new service was a success, but not without pain. Besides the fact that the new service nearly tore the church apart even though (or maybe because) it grew, Cathy and her husband were also struggling in their marriage. Worship leaders are spiritual leaders. Cathy often looks back on those days to ruefully admit that she was not really the spiritual leader she should have been since her personal and public life were at odds.

The miracle is that God continued to use Cathy and her husband anyway. God led them through their brokenness to call Cathy into ordained ministry, healing their marriage along the way and growing Cathy into a true worshiper in the process. Her journey provided a life that is much more consistent within itself than it was before Cathy recognized she was even on a worship journey!

God also showed Cathy her vocational calling of starting

---

[9] In his book, Dynamic Worship, Ken Callahan says, Mission is worship; Worship is mission. p. 88, Dynamic Worship: Mission, Grace, Praise and Power (c) 1994, Kennon L. Callahan, Jossey-Bass Publishers, San Francisco

[10] Missional Worship: Increasing Attendance and Expanding the Bounda-ries of the Church, ibid

worship services and starting churches through this worship journey. Cathy is eternally grateful.

## THE BIBLICAL THEME OF WORSHIP: God's Story

Worship is mission.[9] It is a journey with a destination: to find ourselves in God. God designed the journey and gives all of us plenty of opportunity to get on the journey and plenty of room not to get it, too. When we go on the journey, we often realize we have been on the journey for a long time already. We find that God's story intertwines with our story. Our story is one often of resisting the journey and then eventually going on the journey wholeheartedly. God's story is goodness; our story is seeking after God's goodness. The worship journey is the recognition of God's story and our story intertwining. We are transformed through God's love, through our worship of God. We find ourselves through this journey because we have found God.

**Note:** *Cathy's journey and the description of this worship journey, above, is one of our construction fundamentals of transformation of the heart (stringers). Cathy's transformation was as an upfront leader. The worship journey of the upfront leader impacts and promotes transformation of the hearts of all persons in seats. Cathy's story also provides an inkling for how a passion for Jesus is more important than the raw musical talent of the upfront leader.*

In 2007, Cathy wrote a book called *Missional Worship*[10] in which she distinguishes between our worship relationship with God, 24/7, and the worship service (aka the gusset plate), an hour a week. *Building Worship Bridges*, the book, is largely about the one-hour per week. But *Building Worship Bridges*, the behavior, grows from our 24/7 relationship with God. We worship our way into *Building Worship Bridges* through the identification, pursuit, telling and retelling of God's story and the way it intertwines with our own stories of transformation. The way we live our lives and our desire and practice of making new disciples are the evidence that God is real to us. This is the roadway in our bridge metaphor – the worship journey. As we noted in Part One, Chapter One, the worship service is where we publicly celebrate our transformation. The service also provides the impetus to continue our work of discipleship – our own, and our calling to make new disciples of Jesus Christ. We are on a two-way worship road supported by the missional focus (the footings) and the piers (discipleship). The worship relationship with God and the worship service (gusset plates) are intrinsically connected. Worship is God's story; therefore, it is ours, too.

At the center of God's and our intertwining stories is Jesus Christ. God's biblical theme of worship is tied to God's biblical theme of salvation. Salvation is the impact of God's desire to bring goodness into human lives and our openness and willingness to receive that goodness. For Christians, the dovetailing of God's story and ours happens though Jesus Christ. Jesus is our savior and the object of our affection. Jesus Christ saves us from our wandering ways and brings us back to God, to grow as disciples.

### Worship journeys and the biblical theme of salvation

The Bible speaks frequently about Jesus' role in "saving" humanity. Jesus came:

- to find and restore the lost
  **Luke 19:10** (MSG)
- so they can have real and eternal life, more and better life than they ever dreamed of.
  **John 10:10** (MSG)

Mainliners struggle with the concept of salvation because of traditional explanations from evangelical and non-denominational churches. Here are some of the concepts mainliners might struggle with around the theme of salvation.

- If we are saved from something, it is sin.

- If we are sinners, we are potentially bound to eternal damnation or hell.

- The only way out of hell is belief in Jesus.

- We only get to heaven after we die by believing in Jesus.

- God is distant and available to us only through Jesus.

For many mainliners, these explanations are too stark and many mainliners ignore the topic. We, the authors, find that not dealing with the topic of salvation has watered down the Christian message in many mainline churches. If you do not talk about salvation publicly (in sermons, conversations, small groups, worship services, and other venues of church life), your church will be nothing more than another self-help organization. The worship bridge we are building is a Christian bridge because we are Christ followers. Here are some of our (the authors') thoughts on the topic of salvation:

**Creation.** Bishop Farr points out that God created humankind with a God-sized hole in us that God wants us to fill with Jesus, because God is longing for a relationship with us. So, God designed us with the capacity and yearning for that relationship. We humans are going to worship something – anything, because the capacity and yearning are there through creation. If we miss Jesus we will fill the hole with false idols. (Kay suggests that the word "idol" becomes "the doll of I". Twisted!) Filling the hole with false idols is the same as worshiping the idol. Worshiping idols is a cover-up for our "lost-ness." Idols include our bodies, cars, academics, kids, kids' sports, jobs, income, anger, pride, boredom and addictions. Worshiping Jesus makes it difficult to worship idols because God fills the God-sized hole through our worship of God. We loosen our grip on idolatry. Positivity and hope follow.

**Fully human.** Cathy finds that through our worship of God, God is showing us that we are not God. In the Garden of Eden, the man and the woman wanted to be God-like. The drive to try to be God-like is a drive to control life's outcomes. Realizing that only God is God — and we are not — helps us recognize that only God has power over outcomes. That awareness leaves us completely free to be fully human and thus to worship Christ alone. Worship teaches us to be us.

**Christian community.** We, the authors, wonder if God might be trying to save us for something more than from something. What if God is saving us for community and healthy relationships? When we are growing toward transformation, we are better able to live in peace with others. Worship is our venue.

**Eternity.** Christians fundamentally believe in God's eternal nature. Some of us are less concerned about what happens after we die than we are with what happens while we are living upon this earth: "the Kingdom of heaven is at hand." It is the Christian belief in the eternal nature of God that changes how we live our lives on this earth. Worship gives us peace in the moment without worrying about something we have no control over (death).

**Calling.** The worship journey (the two-way roadway) and the worship service (gusset plates) are symbiotically connected. Worshipers of Jesus Christ on the worship journey are following God into the mission field for that is where God always leads Christ followers. The new people we meet may want to learn about Jesus, too, so we invite them to the worship service. The worship journey leads to the worship service and the worship service leads to the worship journey. That two-way-road intrinsic relationship between journey and gathering helps us see the rhythm of life, in which we are players whose very existence impacts the grand scheme of things.

# TECHNICAL CONSTRUCTION

## PRINCIPLE #1:
## TELL GOD'S STORY

There are many ways you can tell God's story of worship and salvation. The point is that you tell it because it is compelling for new and old alike. Story-telling is a competency requiring study and training – especially when it comes to the worship service. We gain our own experiences of God in life on our worship journey. We learn how to organically translate those authentic stories into various worship forms in the worship service (liturgies, music, preaching, communion, more ...). Worship designers and upfront leaders strive to make worship service components competent and compelling so new people will fit in when they attend and so regulars can worship in spirit and truth.

---

[11] There are numerous ways to get to know your mission field, including prayer walks, community leader interviews, focus groups, and an excel-lent demographic tool called MissionInsite, http://missioninsite.com/ MissionInsite is an excellent tool for finding out details about your mission field. We urge you, however, not to rely solely on any demographic study for knowing your context. Demographic studies are about statis-tics, and worship and outreach are about the heart. You must get out into your mission field to get to know your context personally so that your heart literally breaks for persons who might not have a relationship with Christ or the Christian church. Use your demographic study to con-firm your personal insights.

*Learning to tell God's story directly bridges us to making technical changes in our churches to continue to encourage the already convinced and to make the existing service a place that new people want to come to also.*

A side-note for those starting new services: Your service will not be new forever! You will form traditions quickly. You can head off staleness by instilling continuous transformation (the stringers) and quality (the floor beams) as fundamental values early on in your formation of your new service. Continuously find new ways to make your worship service competent and compelling from day one!

## PREPARING YOUR CHURCH FOR GUESTS:
### Teach Worship (to tell God's story)

Let us not get caught up in thinking that we can make technical changes and suddenly everyone will be flocking to our churches! Let's remember that the most important technical changes you make in your service will grow out of your relationship with your mission field. [11] The authentic interaction we have with the mission field impacts the way we design and lead public worship to welcome them - not as much to attract them. Consider these suggestions for helping your church prepare for guests:

**God is in charge.** The miracle of public worship is that God can use the praises of Christ followers and even the seeking and wondering of non-believers in the gathered community to influence others toward faith in Christ. There is a power in public worship we do not see elsewhere because of the corporate nature of it. That power is palpable for worship leaders and thus tempting. We are tempted to design worship services for the purpose of influencing new persons toward faith. That is not our job; it's God's job.

Imbibing on God's power makes the worship experience forced and "all about me" and may appear inauthentic.

**Worship leaders design public worship with new people in mind so new people can fit in but not so that we can force someone new to believe.** When new people fit in, it is often not long before they begin to raise their arms, eyes, and hearts heavenward. That moment in time may be the first recognition for the guest that they even have a story of growing faith in God. Secondly, it may be the first time they realize that their story also connects with God's story and the stories of the faith community. But we who design and lead worship cannot control that outcome. The guest might not connect. Amen.

**Our own authentic praises of God teach worship.** The only power worship leaders have unlimited access to comes through our own surrender – our own authentic praises of God. The church is called to teach worship and we teach worship by worshiping. Pause a moment to consider this concept.

## Teach how to worship in the worship service by worshiping

In the worship service, we all tell God's story and our stories through public expressions of praise (singing, praying, scripture, confession, forgiveness, etc.). Persons in seats usually do not utter spontaneous thought aloud. We communicate loudly through our behavior. A new person can see that something has happened to us to cause us to be focusing on God overtly.

We are not paying attention to the new person to see if they notice us when we are engaged in worship. We care only that God sees us. Church leaders are responsible for teaching this deep value to persons in seats about public worship. We should all be thrilled that guests attend, but then we should just worship when they do. That is how they will learn to worship, too.

**THE GUEST EXPERIENCE:** *Everyone Has a Story*

Like Bishop Farr always says, "You never know what has happened in someone's life the week before they showed up on Sunday."[12] Your guest has a story, too. He will learn to tell his story in the context of God's story. The search to find meaning and understand "self" is built into our human condition (DNA). We know this because worship leads us to those discoveries. We, the church, must come to understand and believe that our guests attend worship looking for a way to fill up that God-sized worship hole.

### A Guest's Experience

*It was a rough night last night and you felt like crap and did not want to get up. You left the kids at your mom's last night and you still had to pick them up this morning on time. You have been struggling with how much you party sometimes. It seems like the people you hang out with are a bad influence yet you keep hanging out because it distracts you from the struggle of being a single parent. When you can leave the kids with your mom it frees you up. But the effect is only temporary. It is right back to reality in the morning right along with the bottle flu.*

*It's not like it was an impulsive decision, but it still seemed random to just decide right then you were going to go to church this morning. You had been thinking about it for a while but never pulled the trigger. Maybe ... just maybe the church will provide some answers. Some friends had invited you to their church but you never took them up on it. Today it just seemed like you should go.*

---

[12] The majority of new people that will join your church will be transfers; this is true of any size church. See Stetzer's article on Debunking Mega Church Myths, http://www.christianitytoday.com/edstetzer/2013/february/debunking-megachurch-myths-especially-one-about-sheep.html. This fact does not suggest that we should ignore unchurched persons, or discount the possibility that someone will drop in. We wonder, too, if transfers find their way to churches that plan and lead worship for the guest because it is more relevant for the transfers just like it's more relevant for the per-son without much Christian experience. A transfer is still a guest when they attend a church for the first time.

*You decided not to go to your friend's church; maybe you'd have to tell them why you suddenly felt moved if you did. There is this church near your house that looks a lot like the one you grew up in. You surprised even yourself as you got into your car, drove to your mom's a few blocks away, picked up your kids and then drove to the church near your house arriving just before the service started.*

*When you walked in, you were greeted by someone wearing a plastic name tag. She gave you a paper name tag (which you did not want to wear for so many reasons). Then she started asking you about your church background and if both kids were yours. That pissed you off. You knew her questioning was because your younger one had a different color skin than your older one. You ignored the question and inquired if there was a place to take your kids during the service.*

*The woman told you there was nothing because kids should be in the service so they would learn how to behave in church. You looked around the room where the band was and did not see any other kids besides your own. In fact, there were not many people at all. The room felt too big for the crowd. But, you still took your kids in and sat down.*

*As you sat there listening to announcements drone on, you wondered if you yourself knew how to behave in church. Then the music started and people in the room stood but didn't sing. The singers up front were all holding mics and were super enthusiastic, but it seemed fake. They did not sound that good. It was cheesy and kind of depressing.*

*As you sat there, you felt sad. None of it was what you were looking for. It all reminded you of the church you grew up in. Like a nightmare, only it's daytime. Maybe a "daymare." Too much like the past and you were trying to get over your past. So almost right after the music started, you grabbed your kids and left. Never to return. On the way out, your older one said, "Wow mom. That was creepy!" Totally!*

**GUEST EXPERIENCE DEBRIEF:** *The Story Exchange*

In our made-up-but-based-in-reality story, our guest must learn to tell her story to grow spiritually. The guest had a God-sized hole she was looking to fill. Yet, she left the church with the same hole and maybe a bit bigger. She was seeking hope and answers but all she found was awkwardness and uneasiness. The church's role is to try to help the guest tell her story through worship. That means a guest must be able to connect to the way we do things (to tell her story in our context). Even if we do as much as possible to remove obstacles (datedness, poor quality) that could impede a guest's connection, the guest still might not connect.

Here is the point: We do not give a guest a chance to even say no (let alone yes) when we do nothing to change our clunky, churchy communication styles. First time guests make up their minds very quickly about coming back to your church - sometimes within just a few minutes of being there.[13] The "no" was predetermined in our made-up-but-based-in-reality guest story because the church never told their story.

Or did the church tell a different story than they intended? This is the question we should be asking ourselves about our churches. In our made-up-but-based-in-reality story, the church told a story of disengagement and suspicion. The greeter showed distrust with inappropriate questions of the guest. The congregation exhibited disengagement by not participating in the service (no singing), and by their low attendance numbers (among other things you will notice as you read on).

Disengagement in your service communicates disengagement from God to your guests. The smallest things communicate volumes, so pay attention! In the case of our made-up-but-based-in-reality story, too many things happened at the beginning of

---

[13] LifeWay Research; http://www.lifeway.com/Article/How-to-get-first-time-guests-to-come-back

the guest's experience at *Decelerating Church* that soured her, taking away any opportunity for her to get in touch with her own story (in that context). Let's take a look at what may not be helpful for building worship bridges:

**The decision to come to church.** A lot went on in our guest's mind before she decided to come to church, perhaps for weeks or months before she finally attended. Something pushed her forward now. Maybe it was that God-sized hole.

> **The fix:** *Stop to think about it.* It does not matter if we do not know what drove a guest to our front door. It matters that we recognize that it probably took a lot for your guest to finally opt-in. Awareness grows compassion for others' journeys. Your compassion will change the way you plan and lead the public worship experience (so true).

**The wrong greeter.** The person that greeted the guest grilled her and even asked the guest a personal and inappropriate question about whether both kids were hers resulting in belying a level of prejudice. The greeter also gave the guest unwanted advice on child-rearing (to take them into the worship service so they would learn how to behave in church) instead of making her and her family feel like they could fit in.

> **The fix:** *Learn about spiritual gifts.* Welcoming new people is not about placing warm bodies in jobs that need to get done. Instead, consider including a spiritual gift inventory in your discipleship process[14] to help people serve where God intended. Additionally, some churches neglect to train greeters and ushers in being hospitable for today's culture. Greeting should be more about relationships

---

14 Most Mainline Churches do not have a discipleship process, or faith formation plan to follow. Look to Kay Kotan's work and leadership in the book Gear Up. Some use Phil Maynard's work in his book Shift.

than it is about having a "job" on Sunday. All spiritual gifts are hospitable when we use then naturally:

> Be generous with the different things God gave you, passing them around so all get in on it: if words, let it be God's words; if help, let it be God's hearty help. That way, God's bright presence will be evident in everything through Jesus, and he'll get all the credit as the One mighty in everything—encores to the end of time. Oh, yes!
>
> **1 Peter 4: 9-10** (MSG)

**Misuse of name tags.** At *Decelerating Church*, greeters give guests paper name tags as though it is the epitome of welcoming. Today's guest may not want to give you their name yet. If regulars are wearing plastic name tags and the only person that is wearing a paper one is the new person, the guest sticks out like a sore thumb.

> **The fix:** *Standardize name tag usage.* Perhaps you might give your guest the option of whether they want a matching name tag if most people are wearing the paper ones. At *Accelerating Church*, you might see only official greeters or connectors wearing plastic name tags. No one else wears any name tag because it is increasingly difficult to make sure everyone is identified by name at a growing church. The most difficult part of plastic nametags is the location of the name tag rack, especially when it is situated in a place that impedes traffic flow. At *Decelerating Church*, trying to move that name tag rack can cause mutiny. Name tags and the name tag rack is the wrong thing to be fighting over. Begin the discussion about whether to use nametags in your church considering the guest perspective.

**Teaching kids to behave in church.** Churches that espouse the value that kids should be in adult worship so that they learn to behave in church typically have very few kids in their churches. We find there are two primary reasons why.

**One:** The two-hour church culture (one for the worship service and one for Sunday School) is not culturally friendly to new people in most contexts. We will talk about this more in the next chapter.

**Two:** Teaching kids to behave in church is a church person's value, not a new person's value. New people have no clue themselves how to behave in church. At *Accelerating Church,* you will find children's church or "kids'-own" worship (aka *Kid Zone Worship*) concurrently with the worship service. This means families are at church for just one hour (not two). You might consider including kids in the opening praise set during the service and then sending them to some type of children's church when that is over. This way, they can see their parents praising God and praying but then be released to learn about God in age appropriate venues. The expectation of kids in *Decelerating Church* is often for them to behave like adults in a venue designed for adults.

**The fix:** Sleuth! Send a couple young families to churches known for kid's ministries during Sunday worship. Make sure the families take their kids so that the kids can say what they liked about it. And make sure the parents are devoted to seeing your church grow (lest they decide to jump ship over to *Accelerating Church*). Learn what you can from their experience. Then develop your ministry contextually doing whatever you can do right now to welcome kids in a relevant way.

**Lack of critical mass.** The guest walked into a room that was too big for the number of people in it. We call that the cringe factor.

If you are starting a new service or trying to salvage an existing one, find a space to meet that feels fuller when you gather. Or consider creative room design to seemingly shrink the space.

> **The fix:** Shrink your space and/or work with a coach. Fixing your space creatively might mean adding artistically designed kiosk type banners that you position toward the front of the room (and everyone sits in front of those banners). It might mean removing pews or perhaps re-spacing them. Try creating a hospitality space at the back of the worship space / sanctuary (especially if you have taken out pews). These are a few suggestions. What other ideas do these suggestions trigger? If your worship service has declined to a very low number, you might be looking at a different solution than adjusting room size. We, the authors, would speculate (based on our experiences and observations) that attendance less than 50% capacity indicates a need to address critical mass or perhaps start over. To start over, hire a coach!

**Poor music quality.** Quality is a worship gap at *Decelerating Church*. The use of technology in our secular culture has influenced us all to expect high quality in music and hospitality everywhere. Go to your shopping mall or local restaurant or gym. Our churches must value quality in that same way. More about quality in the next chapter.

> **The fix:** *Read and implement the suggestions in Chapter Two!*

**Misplacement and misunderstanding of announcements.** We all know it! Announcements are not guest friendly at *Decelerating Church*. But many of us do not know why and we do not know what to do to make them more relevant.

> The fix: Read Chapter three! We will help you know why

announcements do not work in most of our churches. We will also teach how to use announcements in a way that communicate something of value about your church to your guest.

## ADAPTIVE CONSTRUCTION

**PRINCIPLE #1:**
**TELL YOUR STORY**

*"It's who you are and the way you live that count before God. Your worship must engage your spirit in the pursuit of truth. That's the kind of people the Father is out looking for: those who are simply and honestly themselves before him in their worship. God is sheer being itself—Spirit. Those who worship Him must do it out of their very being, their spirits, their true selves, in adoration."*

**John 4:23-24 (MSG)**

The Christian church teaches worship by worshiping. When committed Christ followers gather to worship God, we tell God's story and we also tell our own stories. Others see that there is a story because we are worshiping in spirit and in truth. That is how the worship service becomes an environment in which new people can learn they too have a story they need to tell (through worshiping God).

It is the role of upfront worship leaders to help persons in seats tell their own authentic stories of worship by telling our own authentic stories of worship. Our public praises of God that grow from our deep, personal relationship with God are the number one bridge-building tool we have. Public praises include singing, praying, reading scripture, speaking liturgies, confessing, forgiving, listening and considering what is going on around us. Public praises also include any upfront leadership role we have, like choir directing, preaching, or leading congregational singing.

Public praises also include the spontaneous or sometimes planned moments in the worship service when we use our upfront role to usher persons in seats into the presence of Christ. We do that through our own words of personal confession about where God is right now in our lives. Those small, confessional times and the words we use are powerfully influential for persons in seats. Public leaders help persons in seats recognize that their authentic worship of God is important to God and to the community often through their own struggles. Authentic, transparent public leadership done well (without being needy) impacts the gathered community (so important!).

### PREPARE YOURSELF FOR GUESTS: Surrender

Upfront worship leaders are upfront because of their spiritual gifts and their heart for Jesus (calling). Being upfront gives a person visibility and influence over persons in seats toward their spiritual journey. Influence demands responsibility. The responsibility is for upfront leaders to be in a serious worship journey 24/7.

This worship journey will impact how we read (if we are liturgists), how we direct (if we are musicians) and how we plan (if we are behind the scenes worship designers). The worship journey is critical because of the dynamics that upfront leadership creates, both positively and negatively.

*Building Worship Bridges* will cause persons in seats to look to you (the upfront leader) for spiritual guidance. It will also draw push-back. That is the nature of spiritual leadership: forward spiritual motion draws an opposite and equal reaction. Some refer to that as "spiritual warfare." In whatever way you define or label it, it is not possible to be an upfront spiritual leader without encountering negativity.

The challenge is great for this high calling. No behind the scenes or upfront leader can waffle in the face of push-back. Our purpose is missional. It will be difficult to withstand the pressure. We cannot do it on our own. We need God. We who are public leaders need most to surrender to God. When we surrender to God behind the scenes, we can authentically teach surrender to the congregation during worship. That is how congregations change.

When we allow the inevitable push-back within the system to stop us in our tracks, it is evidence that our private and public lives are not in sync. That makes it very difficult to teach worship by worshiping, because authenticity is missing. None of us are perfect; this is a journey. That is why leaders must continuously and publicly confess and forgive through our worship and our intentional public leadership.

Our own surrender to God keeps us grounded. Many spiritual leaders are not practicing the presence of Christ in their own lives to the degree they need to in order to tell their own stories authentically. When there is this disconnect, the spiritual leaders are unable to produce powerful public worship experiences. We cannot give away what we do not have.

### THE LEADER EXPERIENCE: *Worship Leaders Live Real Lives*

Like Cathy always says, "You never know what has happened in the worship leader's life in the week – or the hour – before they showed up on Sunday." Whatever that event is, it is always difficult to shake from the leader's thoughts before going into a worship service.

The worship leader's focal point is to help others make sense of the experience. How we handle life's curve balls publicly is part of our authenticity or part of our cover up.

### *A Leader's Experience*

*Your alarm rang loudly and practically made you jump. It was time to get up to go to your worship leading gig at Decelerating Church. How depressing! You were going to have to be all rah-rah about God as you stood in front of the congregation. It wasn't going to do any good. No one there would feel anything anyway — including you.*

*Your worship service at Decelerating Church was lame. It seemed like a Herculean task to try to make it better. You did not even know if you had the energy for it. It would be easier to just quit. Maybe Accelerating Church would hire you. You felt very jealous of all their success. Why haven't I been given the opportunity to be known like their worship leader is known? Why haven't I been able to get some of my songs published? That guy's stuff isn't that much better than mine, is it? You questioned if God even loved you and wanted to use you. You felt like you had so much talent to share.*

*While you were driving to Decelerating Church, your thoughts would not leave you alone. You cried out loud to God as though it was God's fault. "Why are there not better musicians at our church? Why is our pastor's preaching so bad? Why is everyone so unwilling to do anything new?"*

*You felt yourself growing angry about the situation your church has put you into ... leading a dying congregation with the expectation of it being your sole responsibility to make it somehow magically grow. Leading worship that morning was not good, you were so pissed. It was a waste of time. Same thing different Sunday. You left hoping something would happen to get you out of there.*

**LEADER EXPERIENCE DEBRIEF:** *True Story*

We three writers have felt we were going through the motions of spiritual leadership at different times. It does not feel good! But we, the authors, have learned that we do not have to entirely hide our disconnectedness from persons in seats. Many others in the gathered community feel disconnected from God, too. Worship leadership is about seeking God anyway and helping others do the same even when doing so seems futile. Let's now take a look at the unhealthy practices to notice in the leader story:

**Having to be all "rah-rah" about God.** When worship leadership feels forced, it is a sign of a disconnect between us (the leader) and God. When we stay connected to the vine, it is less likely we will feel forced to be "rah-rah." More than that, we just must be real that we are human beings and that sometimes we will not know God is there.

> **The fix:** *Spending time with God.* Spending time with God is a discipline that we will discuss more in the next chapter. Learning to speak plainly in your public role about your own humanity is a skill that we will introduce soon. To tie this back to our construction fundamentals, spending time with God is the discipleship pier.

**Competing with** *Accelerating Church.* We writers have identified competitive emotions in ourselves at different times in our leadership. Perhaps you can relate.

> **The fix:** *Be who you are.* One of the most profound truths about following God is that it makes us who we are, not someone we are not. All worship leaders can reach some people but not all people. You will gain more traction in *Building Worship Bridges* when you worry about connecting with those that are receptive to you. *Accelerating Church* keeps pushing forward from the place where they are right now.

**Revealing your journey.** It is part of our calling as spiritual leaders.

> **The fix:** *Develop a personal story (testimony).* In our story above, our spiritual leader was in a spiritual crisis. Biblically, that is a common reality. Read the Psalms! When a

spiritual leader in crisis surrenders to God, it deepens the worship experience and offers the ability to lead others who may also be in spiritual crisis. That does not happen without intentionality. In the case of our protagonist in The Leader Experience story, we did not hear if the spiritual leader was practicing ways to fill up his empty soul. We did hear him lash out and get angry. Did he even consider speaking about his inner turmoil in a way that would reveal he is human and help people in turmoil recognize that turmoil is part of our stories? God takes us from where we are and grows us from that point.

**CONSTRUCTION TIME**
**GO TO THE WORKBOOK: Part Two, Chapter Five, Phase One**

Learning to tell your worship story in different ways, including through actions and words, is a foundational tool in *Building Worship Bridges*. It is skill development. Where should you insert your ideas? How long should you speak? What should you say? We answer those questions when we learn to think about the worship order anew. We recommend going to the workbook now to absorb the teaching on worship orders. It will greatly impact the way you work through *Building Worship Bridges*.

# Chapter Six _____

## Phase Two: Hospitality

In August, 2015, Bishop Farr heard Tony Campolo speak in Missouri at Compass Pastor's Leadership Training. Tony talked about how the worship wars are not Biblical. He said that the church has always had to adapt to different forms of worship and music.

He pointed out that trying to solve the worship wars by having separate but equal styles of worship (one "contemporary" one "traditional" service) does not help long-time church members grow. It keeps us from experiencing new music styles. It also does not help newcomers cherish the depth of insight into God that traditional hymnody teaches. Tony shared this scripture:

> *He said, "Then you see how every student well-trained in God's kingdom is like the owner of a general store who can put his hands on anything you need, old or new, exactly when you need it."*
> **Matthew 13:52** (MSG)

We, the authors, interpret Tony's comments this way:

- Hospitality is part of God's story and thus is an umbrella of holiness for the church. The worship wars are inhospitable thus not Godly.
- When we tell God's hospitality story in a way new people understand it using new forms of music as well as other new forms of welcoming, we tell our (the church's) hospitality story of generosity.
- Telling the church's story of generosity means that the church is open to change, since hospitality changes as culture changes (back to the stringer metaphor). Even if you are starting a new service, it will no longer be new at some point. Continuous change is inevitable in any worship service if you want to continuously welcome new people.

## Hospitality is the opposite of the worship wars

When churches fight over introducing new music, they often fight over a couple other aspects of hospitality, too. Besides music, the two other common areas churches fight over include kids' ministries and acts of welcoming. We, the authors, refer to these three areas of hospitality as The THREE BIG WOWS (the trusses). They are central to your ability to help new people fit in. Fights over any one of the Wows constitute the worship wars. If we want to gain traction *Building Worship Bridges*, our churches need the full complement of hospitality offered in current, relevant ways, without bitterness or blame.

The worship wars exist in churches everywhere – even larger churches. Some churches are still large when signs of aging and decline creep in. Perhaps the church has been thinking, *if it ain't broke, don't fix it.* The church may have a few different services that are not large individually, though they create a collective larger number overall. Attenders are hunkered down in their time slot. The "contemporary" service in that church is dated and new and more diverse populations do not get it. The "traditional" service in that church is not growing and serves only much older people. The larger church has tried a very new style of worship and it flopped, because there was no attention to invitation and outreach. Trying to change any one of those environments results in regular attenders digging in their heels and refusing change, because the church has not taught nor practiced the missional focus (footings), quality and change (beams and stringers).

Churches die over worship wars since new people do not want to be around crabby churches and crabby people.

Starting another service to stop the worship wars is a band aid to a larger problem: lack of devotion to God's story of hospitality. And likely, without a missional focus, there will be no one to attend a new worship service because the church is not reaching new people.

## THE BIBLICAL THEME OF HOSPITALITY: *Generosity*

Hospitality is part of God's story; learn to tell it! In doing so, you will tell your own story of generosity. The Bible repeatedly refers to the importance of welcoming the stranger, often implying that we welcome the company of heaven when we welcome those we do not know and are not like us:

> *Don't forget to show hospitality to strangers, for some who have done this have entertained angels without realizing it!*
> **Hebrews 13:2** (MSG)

How far are you willing to bend over backwards to welcome the angels God sends your way so that you can be like Jesus and help others learn about and be like Jesus too? Get ready for Olympic-caliber athletic feats! Many of us still behave like it's 1950, 1980, or even 1999.[15] It is much easier for new people to fit in when you fulfill the bridge-building fundamental of change (stringers) by developing culturally relevant acts of welcoming, current kids' ministries, and fun new music.

### Comparing current hospitality trends to dated ones

In 1950, and even in 1980, hospitality occurred in the fellowship hall after the service with cookies and weak, generic coffee served in china cups that hold about four ounces.

**Acts of welcoming** at *Accelerating Church* begin during the Gathering time (actually they start on their website and social media) before the actual start of the Praise segment. (Note: if you have not looked at the workbook yet, you will need to under-

---

[15] Cathy is from Minnesota and could not resist her Prince homage with the 1999 reference. However, it is true that we are nearly 20 years after the turn of the century as we write this book. Some churches have started worship services that date back that far and have not yet introduced change and have not yet responded to a changing mission field. Mission fields change regularly. When we notice the change in our churches it is often too late. How are you keeping up with your changing mission field? What have you done to update your worship service in the past twenty years? In the past ten years? In the past five?

77

stand this chapter and beyond.)

For our current culture, it is too late to wait until after the service is over to begin the welcoming process. At *Accelerating Church*, forget about the cookies and concentrate on the coffee. Serve a flavorful local brand before the service in a minimum of eight-ounce insulated cups with a lid so we can take it into the worship space. If you are urban, make the coffee fair trade.[16]

Don't forget flavored teas and soda (pop!). *Accelerating Church* also makes sure guests know where they are going (signage outside the building and inside of the building). There are no piles of clutter in various corners. No need to keep objects someone donated fifty years prior (with the gold plate still attached), although there may be a dedicated history room with memorabilia of years past and community memories. If the meeting place is not completely new, it is at least updated. The building or meeting place at *Accelerating Church* is compelling like the worship service.

**Kid's ministries** at *Accelerating Church* are safe, professional, lively and content rich about Jesus - since our current culture is very concerned about our kids! *Accelerating Church* provides professionally staffed nurseries with background checked workers. Teenage volunteers will not do without the guidance of the professionals alongside them.

Parents register infants through grade-school age kids before the service starts. Parents are comfortable leaving their kids in areas that are engaging and safe for kids with plenty of adults manning the fort.

Teaching is delivered by video; teachers learn from the videos and help kids grasp the meaning. There may be an activity to reinforce the learning. Children's church occurs at the

---

[16] To find out about fair trade coffee, go to https://en.wikipedia.org/wiki/Fair_trade_coffee

same time as adult worship. *Accelerating Church* does not expect parents to be in church for more than one hour on a Sunday morning. *Accelerating Church* recognizes that very few new people will connect to a two-hour culture because new people already think they have given the entire morning by attending a one-hour long worship service.

**Music** at *Accelerating Church* is consistent, current and high quality. You hear recorded background music in the lobby. Background music facilitates comfort for the guest who is often nervous or apprehensive about attending church. Music starts about twenty minutes before the service starts. You can hear it throughout the building and even in the worship space. *Accelerating Church* grasps that music is cultural and an identifier of the church.

Guests will not listen to poor quality music, so *Accelerating Church* makes sure their music is high quality from beginning to end. Recorded background music starts up again as the service ends. Recorded music is contemporary. Worship music is often contemporary, too, and always high quality. Did we mention the music at *Accelerating Church* is always high quality?

**First impressions: The THREE BIG WOWS**

Just like the trusses of the bridge are the most visible part of the bridge, the three Wows are the most visible parts of any worship service and must be done well and with cultural relevance for a church to be truly welcoming to a guest. The WOWS are part of the infrastructure of your worship bridges. Without these hospitality trusses, you would have nothing for the road-bed to be built upon.

In worship design, we see The THREE BIG WOWS, but do not see the missional focus (the footings) or the intentional discipleship (piers), but they must be present to support the worship journey (the roadway). Trust us, the missional focus is there in a church that is gaining traction!

Unfortunately, you know and we know that churches can have a missional focus and still operate superficially. We need excellent and culturally relevant first impressions so guests can fit in and possibly then learn about Jesus. But paying attention to first impressions can still come off "fake." It would be like going into a clothing store with the background music playing, the sales people smiling, giving you a bottle of water, and then pushing clothing on you so that you buy-buy-buy.

The THREE BIG WOWS do not automatically help new people "buy" Christianity or "buy" your church. If we are using the three Wows to try to trick people into either of those two choices, we are not real. Even in 1950, people knew whether you wanted them there or whether your actions were bait and switch. Ideally, the work you do to improve first impressions is authentic and leads to true relationships.

But we, the church, still must let people choose our church and even choose Christianity. Even God does not force those choices.

First impressions are about understanding how people connect. When we ask people in our seminars what they think the THREE BIG WOWS are, almost always someone shouts out, preaching. Preaching is important.

Maybe it is the fourth BIG WOW. For sure, a person that wants to grow in faith wants to hear a well- spoken sermon that challenges and guides them. That sermon will bring them back.

But in most cases, the sermon occurs in the latter half of the worship service and first-time guests decide to return more often toward the beginning because of the way they perceived your church right off the bat, good or bad. So even if the pastor knocks the sermon out of the park, it is not going to make up for out of date or pushy hospitality at the front end of your service.

# TECHNICAL CONSTRUCTION

## PRINCIPLE #2:
## PAY ATTENTION TO
## FIRST IMPRESSIONS

We have laid out this book in sequence. To make worship changes in your church, you must grasp why we need to make those changes – because of the failed worship bridge (Part One). Then you must recognize that worship is the telling of God's story, and our own stories (Chapter Five). We have given you an opportunity to process all that information in the Workbook: *Complete Construction Manual for Building Worship Bridges*. The next most important area for you to concentrate on is the THREE BIG WOWS. They are like low-hanging fruit on a technical level. We gain traction on church growth getting good at The Three Wows.

### The buzz factor of the THREE BIG WOWS

When guests connect through the Three Wows, it helps increase the traffic flow on your worship bridge. The THREE BIG WOWS become your cultural identity in your area because your guest gives your church exposure when they talk with their friends about their great experience (through the Three Wows).

New people will come to a church they have heard about that has a good reputation. They will attend your church especially if their friend invites them because they like their friend and their friend is endorsing your environment to them. Or they might just show up on your church's doorstep one day because they heard about your church somewhere along the line. The THREE BIG WOWS boost your church's reputation in the neighborhood, unless they are not offered with high quality and in a culturally relevant way for your guest. Then the THREE BIG WOWS become great big UH-OH's.

When WOWS are UH-OH's, the unfulfilled guest will not talk about your church to their friends; you will not have a bad reputation. You will have no reputation. The isolated church is invisible to the mission field. Another UH-OH experience may even lead your guest to the confirmation that "church" is the very same as they personally remembered, or heard about the church, from when they grew up: yep, this is why we left and why we should not come back again.

## PREPARE YOUR CHURCH FOR GUESTS: *The Hang-out factor*

None of us that plan and lead worship can ever predict if a new person is going to return to our church just because we are bending over backwards with hospitality before the service starts. We can only remove obstacles to increase the odds that a new person will connect and feel they can hang out with us. Something they determine quickly. Very few of us will invest in relationships that are awkward and difficult to be in. In the church, if we can hang out with you, then we can learn about Jesus from you. When new people attend a church that is a throwback culturally, they will assume that you do not get them. How can they learn about Jesus from you if they must teach you how to understand them?

Do not let the hang-out factor cause you to think 21st Century seekers are not seeking substance and meaning of life. Have you ever noticed a group of millennials standing in a cluster all texting on their phones and not looking at each other? Even the older generation is like that now. We are a culture of parallel relationships, each choosing our own path and walking in tandem with others also choosing their own path. We are so connected that we are disconnected. Do we in the church really think unchurched people have not noticed their own disconnection within their own personal relationships? And have we in the church not really noticed our disconnect with one another?

We are all definitely looking for something more because God created us for more. If you do not believe us, go to your gym or Harley Club. You will find numerous opportunities to do good works in the neighborhood. You will also find opportunities to have fun with people at the club that have interests like yours. Secular organizations grasp the hang-out factor.

## THE GUEST EXPERIENCE: *Breaking Down Walls*

In the previous chapter, we met our guest for the first time and encountered *Decelerating Church* through our Guest Experience. In this chapter, we will see what happens with that same guest when she finds her way to *Accelerating Church*. Note how the Three Wows come into play.

### A guest's experience

*At Accelerating Church, you found yourself drawn into the music right away. You walked in late but didn't feel awkward since the room was full. Everyone was standing and seemed engaged. Only the people in the row you squeezed into noticed you. A few smiled. The upfront leader had a nice voice and the band was so good – like at a concert. You weren't thinking as much about yourself you liked the music so much.*

*It was a completely different experience when you got to Accelerating Church than it was at Decelerating Church earlier that morning. When you walked out at Decelerating Church and drove away you noticed the directional signs for Accelerating Church. It was ironic, so you decided to follow them. You thought it couldn't be any worse there than where you just were. You kept following the signs that led you to the parking lot of Accelerating Church.*

*Once you got there and saw the name, you realized that was your friends' church. That made it easier somehow to consider* going in - especially after *Decelerating Church. Your friends had told you about how fun this church was for them and their kids. You had also noticed some pretty big changes in their lives after going there a while. They had asked you to go with them some time. You had thought about going there this morning but instead went to Decelerating Church. And now here you were!*

*The parking lot was full but not many cars were driving in. You figured you were late, but two people in orange vests smiled and waved. So, you pulled in and they pointed out a spot. When you got to the front door two more people opened it. Then someone else came over to ask you if you wanted to bring your kids into the service or the kids' area. You said the kid's area, so the guy escorted you all the way there. He stayed until your kids were situated. He then walked you back, handed you a cup of coffee, and helped you find a seat in the worship service that had already started. You liked it.*

*Your kids were so excited to go to the kids' area. It was cool looking. The minute you got there they ran into a couple kids they knew from school. The people at the kids' registration desk signed your kids in, took your cell number, and gave you a safety book that explained their policies. It felt good. Your kids didn't even say goodbye! They had already told you they thought their friends went here on the way in.*

### GUEST EXPERIENCE DEBRIEF: *Hospitality Tools and Relationship Impact*

In Chapter One, the Guest Experience at *Decelerating Church* was soured by poor hospitality (aka the THREE BIG WOWS – or should we say Uh-Ohs?) in those first few minutes. The church lost the opportunity for a relationship with our lead character. The *Accelerating Church* experience (this chapter's Guest Experience story) did the opposite. Let's take a look at what may not be helpful for *Building Worship Bridges*:

**Directional Signs**. Our guest followed directional signage to *Accelerating Church*. If someone has decided to come to your church, they know the address and will use their GPS to get there (not your directional signage). Instead, directional signs create anticipation and help guests feel that you are anticipating their arrival. All signage is important to identify and point out your church location. Directional signage is a specific type of signage most churches do not think about. It includes signs in your neighborhood, parking lot, at the front door, and inside the building.

> **The fix:** Research Directional Signs for Churches, perhaps at a church that is using them. On the way to your church, directional signs get put up before your service and taken down after the service every week. A volunteer does this work – NOT the pastor! Use signage from the parking lot to the door where you want people to enter. Wait to invest in signs until after you have implemented enough worship changes to make your environment a place new people will want to attend! Don't forget directional signs in your lobby, too, to help newcomers find bathrooms, kids' area and the worship space. Directional signs in your lobby can become permanent.

**Reputation and Invitation.** It seems like the guest wandered to *Accelerating Church* uninvited. But she really was invited by her friends though she didn't put two and two together until she got there.

> **The fix:** Invitation tools! Google "worship service invitation tools" to find options.

**Greeters and Connectors.** At *Decelerating Church*, we have ushers to help people find seats even when there are too few people to need help being seated. Don't eliminate the usher role just yet; it's an identity for people in long established congregations. Do find a few of your current ushers that can learn how to become greeters and connectors. At *Accelerating Church*, the people with whom we first connect are gifted and equipped (by the church) for their role. They also have a sense of calling by God to serve in this capacity.

They learn to stay at their post early and stay at their post for about ten minutes after the service starts to welcome guests that have been detained. They spontaneously do things to make guests feel comfortable, like the connector did that walked the guest to the kids' area and back again.

**The fix: *Clip In,* by Jim Ozier.**[18] Jim's book will provide tools, techniques and best practices for acts of welcoming. It will help you create an overall culture of radical hospitality for today's world.

*A side-note to Ozier's book:* We, the authors, have been to churches that have excellent music and powerful preaching, but no personal connection to the congregation. For a guest to decide it is worth their time to come back to your church, that personal connection must happen. We have observed low attendance in churches with WOW music and kids but few acts of personal welcoming. WOW hospitality requires all three prongs to be WOW.

**Options.** When the connector came to the guest, he asked her how she wanted to proceed: to the worship space with her kids or to the Kid Zone area. *Accelerating Church* gives choices to the guest. *Decelerating Church* expects the guest to fit in to their way of doing things. Period.

**The fix:** Training and organization. Give your front-line hospitality people the tools and guidance to offer the appro-

---

[18] *Clip In: Risking Hospitality for Your Church*, by Jim Ozier and Fiona Ha-worth © 9/2014, Abingdon Press

priate choices to the guests they interact with.

**Kid Zone Decor, Safety and Teaching.** We spoke about this earlier in this chapter (and in Chapter One).

> **The fix:** Hire or appoint a kid's coordinator, and train. You can send a newly appointed kid's coordinator to a large growing church for training if that church is willing to share what they know about reaching out to kids with you. You may need to send this new coordinator to innovative training outside your area if you do not have a place to learn it locally.

**Coffee in the worship center.** We spoke about this earlier in this chapter. You will need to build buy-in to why you should offer coffee for people to take wherever they go in the building – including into the worship space.

> **The fix:** It's not about the coffee. Do not try to get your church to accept insulated cups with lids so that people can take the coffee into the worship space because you think that is going to bring all sorts of new people. It will not. It will only help you welcome them when they get there so that they can feel like your church is normal. Only the genuine connections you make with people will bring them back. Keep your focus on building relationships to produce true adaptive change.

**Music like a concert.** It is a great complement to a church that a guest thought the church had music comparable to a concert. That means it was culturally relevant and high quality. That is what guests expect with music.

*Decelerating Church* often complains that *Accelerating Church* is "entertaining" people. Research shows that attenders of "entertainment churches" are initially drawn in by the worship and the music. But later they report a higher rate of overall participation in the life of the church and a higher level of spiritual growth. It is the churches that disparage entertainment and that will not change their musical style that also complain the most about how the same people do everything — lack of participation.[19] The Pew study on what makes a church "sticky" corroborates that truth.[20] Churches grow because of discipleship. That truth would apply even to "entertainment" churches.

Great music entertains. Traditional churches would grow with concert-like choir music (and their missional focus, too). "I set myself on fire in hopes that some will come and see," John Wesley, founder of the Methodist Movement.[21] Entertainment is a doorway to participation. It leads us to open our own mouths and praise God with our own voice when it is our turn to sing, if we can sing the songs.

We call your attention to sing-ability. It is so not entertaining when congregational music is hard to sing. Many hymns in our hymnals and supplements are not melodic and much new praise music is also not sing-able for persons in seats. Yet that is the music *Decelerating Church* selects because it is "theme-able" or theologically correct. Cathy has worked with several congregations that have recognized the sing-ability factor. Those churches have changed their music selection to be more participative thus creating more of an entertainment feel in their churches. Surprising!

---

[19] *Not Who You Think They Are: A Profile of the People Who Attend America's Megachurches,* Scott Thumma and Warren Bird; http://hirr.hartsem.edu/megachurch/megachurch_attender_report.htm

[20] 6 Reasons Congregations Have Become Sticky. Forty-nine percent of persons interviewed for the study said they went back because fol-lowing Christ more closely gave them a greater desire to attend church. http://ministrytodaymag.com/outreach/church-growth/23202-6-reasons-congregations-have-become-sticky

[21] The phrase *I set myself on fire in hopes that some might come and see* is attributed to John Wesley, though we cannot find a citation that supports him saying it. At the least, it's folklore with a purpose: it shows us how serious Wesley was about sharing the gospel. If he could enter-tain people enough maybe they'd listen to him about the transforma-tional power of a relationship with Jesus Christ!

[22] Do you think millennials do not like church? Think again. Research shows they are very interested in faith and especially in participating in the development of worship. Interactive is the key – a point we make throughout this book. Read the article: https://www.washingtonpost.com/news/acts-of-faith/wp/2016/09/10/a-new-crop-of-dc-churches-has-discovered-the-secret-to-appealing-to-millennials/

**The fix:** Select sing-able over theme-able music for congrega- tional singing.[22] In our workbook, we have published a list of our Top Seventy-Six most sing-able traditional hymns. We have also provided resources for sing-able contemporary Christian music of different styles. Look at the list to make some fun selections for music your congregation can get into. Then, stop blaming Accelerating Church for their ability to reach new people through their music and instead learn how to improve the quality of your music.

## ADAPTIVE CONSTRUCTION

### PRINCIPLE #2: PAY ATTENTION TO QUALITY

*Do your best. Work from the heart for your real Master, for God, confident that you'll get paid in full when you come into your inheritance.*
**Colossians 3:23** (MSG)

*Accelerating Church* is devoted to high quality. It is important to God as our Bible passage shows us. And it is important to the mission field. Do you by some chance think those two perspectives are connected? Let's stop saying, "It's good enough for church work." When we say that, we are really saying that God, the mission field, and we who are already there do not deserve our best.

### Quality is discerning

Pursuing quality requires that churches have high expectations of "performance." Underneath that expectation is the value that churches appoint leaders and volunteers to serve in their areas of giftedness and passion. Keep in mind that passion trumps giftedness. When giftedness trumps passion and discipleship, it can come off as showmanship and not leading worship. While passion and discipleship is our first priority, giftedness is also required.

Someone with some gifts but who is not a musical expert can learn to maximize their skills when passion for Jesus is present. Driving the idea that we serve in an area of passion and gifting is the understanding that people make lasting relationships with each other when we are "just us." Any time we try to be something we are not, we do not fulfill God's calling. Remember, quality is the floor beams that the worship journey roadway is built upon.

*Decelerating Church* lives with mediocrity. They do not want to hurt anyone's feelings by asking volunteers to improve the way they do things or not to do them. They do not want to ask for excellence from their volunteers because they are volunteers (after all)! We, the authors, can assert that volunteers give a lot of themselves with excellence at *Accelerating Church* because of the called and gifted factor.

*Accelerating Church* is raising up spiritual leaders among laity and staff. Spiritual leaders see themselves as having influence over others to help others grow spiritually. They take their role seriously and are willing to give a lot to fulfill their own calling. Even if they do not get paid for it!

If your church has a low-quality meter, it will likely be difficult to go from an environment in which anything goes to an environment in which you hold the line on doing things better for the sake of helping new people fit in, which also honors God. If we are not able to offer ministry with quality, then perhaps we need to take a step back until we can. Taking a step back can lead to inner turmoil for pastors – even those that do well at leading change.

They will often struggle when they have to raise the bar on quality. Doing so can expose lack of commitment from volunteers and staff. Raising the bar on quality can lead to significant personnel changes throughout your church.

So, take care to work this process forward with courage, compassion and assertiveness. The goal to improve quality is critical to building an enduring worship bridge. We will begin to know we are making progress infusing a missional focus (footings) and discipleship (piers) when someone says, "I am not really that good at doing that. I'm going to take myself out of that and find the place where God has really called and gifted me to serve."

### PREPARE YOURSELF FOR GUESTS: *Gaining buy-in over time*

Spiritual gift inventories will help you raise the bar on quality. You will also find a chart to give you a process for creating buy-in in Chapter Six in the workbook, *Complete Construction Manual for Building Worship Bridges.*

The process of change has a pace to it. It does not rush, nor does it languish. It is steady pressure to keep focusing on the "why," followed by the "what." Do not ever forget to keep telling the worship story, your own, God's, and others'. Worship leaders of all stripes lead the process of change.

Remember, continual transformation (change) is like the stringers that tie into the floor beams to support the worship journey (roadway). A great resource we often recommend to help you think through making changes is a book called *Managing Transitions,* by William Bridges.

But do be aware of one thing that we have already said and will say again: making decisions out of a preference for quality will not work in the face of push back for any area ministry leader if the lead pastor does not own the value of quality first.

The lead pastor reinforces the importance of your congregation's worship story by personally endorsing the move toward quality. That means the lead pastor raises the bar for quality among the staff or ministry area volunteer leaders, who then raise it in their areas of leadership. If the pastor waffles when someone complains because a ministry area leader is demanding more of them, it's all over. Steadfast leadership and commitment are key.

## THE LEADER EXPERIENCE:
### *The Quality Value Equals All-in*

God's story leads to your quality value. Tell God's story and your own story contextually and powerfully because you value quality. It shows whether you are truly all-in for making worship a transformational environment in your church. The all-in factor helps you lead change. You are trying to build an all-in environment for everyone in your church. The more all-in your congregation becomes, the more likely individuals will be able to say, "We will do whatever it takes to make our worship the kind of environment new people want to come to."

If we as leaders are not personally all-in, it will be very difficult to discern if others are or are not all-in. If we cannot discern whether others are all-in, we cannot lead them to become all-in.

### A leader's experience

*While you were worship leading at* **Decelerating Church,** *you saw the Guest get up soon after the music started and walk out. Your stomach sank, but you understood. Why would a new person want to be part of this service the way it is now? You didn't even want to be part of it!*

*As the Guest left, you began to wonder why the congregation was putting up with something that a guest would not seemingly tolerate. Why had you come to tolerate it, you wondered? Why does the pastor tolerate it? Why did the singers and band tolerate it?* **Accelerating Church** *probably wouldn't tolerate it! You* *wondered if the guest would walk out of Accelerating Church that fast. Probably not. You wondered, what was that something that the guest could not tolerate? What are the rest of us ignoring as though it doesn't exist? Your band's level of performance was part of it, for sure. You had to admit that the digital download you listened to of the worship leader's music at* **Accelerating Church** *was awesomely produced. You figured they did that live every week. You were jealous.*

*As you thought about it, you recognized that you were not the most relational person with your team and that you did not put much into training them or asking them for more. You kept playing your music even as the guest left, but the thoughts kept nagging at you. You had never considered the guest before.*

*You looked around the room and saw a dozen people who attended that service because they taught Sunday School during the previous hour. They were there for convenience. The other dozen were people who said they wanted to support this service. But they all went to the other service. With all those cars in the parking lot at* **Accelerating Church,** *people had to be going there for more than just an obligation.*

## LEADER EXPERIENCE DEBRIEF: *Learning not to settle*

In our story, the worship leader started asking questions about why the guest left. It led to deeper questions about the why of worship, though our leader is not grasping what is the question behind his questions. Our worship leader's perspective is superficial. The true why of worship will eventually cause him to not be able to tolerate mediocrity any more – not just for improving the quality but for the inner peace of his own soul. If he doesn't grasp the why, then the why of worship will probably push him out the door to go to work in retail and leave his music behind. When we are going through the motions, we do not endure in much of anything, but especially not church work. Let's now take a look at the unhealthy practices to notice in the leader story:

**You didn't want to be part of this service.**

We have encountered many pastors or other upfront leaders that recognize how rough the worship service is in their church that they are leading. But they do not know what to do about it. We guarantee you, not speaking about it is not the way to go.

> **The fix:** Be truthful about quality. In our workbook is a long list of ways to improve the music in both live band-led and spoken liturgy style services (this is terminology we introduce in the Workbook). If the quality is off, find a way to talk about it with the people that are leading the area that needs improving. Share this book and work through the workbook together. Sometimes bringing in mystery worshippers helps the church see the truth. *Faith Perceptions* specializes in providing this service for churches.[23]

**Developing quality people trumps developing quality music.**

The worship leader was not getting much out of his people. Maybe he wasn't leading them; maybe he didn't have their respect. There is a difference between making something excellent so that "I look good" and trying to lead toward excellence to be faithful and fruitful.

> **The fix:** Do you really care about your people and their relationship with God? People must know you care about them before they will allow you to lead them. Get in touch with your own worship story and start to tell it to gain trust of those you lead. Encourage your team to start sharing their own worship story, too. If you are having trouble growing a

---

[23] http://faithperceptions.com/ Faith Perceptions (FP) is a research organ-ization that gives churches insight into how they are doing reaching new people. FP hires unchurched people to attend a specific church and then tell the truth about the experience; FP collects and docu-ments the information from several mystery guests and then shares it with the church for an honest look at their neighborhood impact from the people they have said they want to reach out to. Melanie Smollen is the president of Faith Perceptions. Melanie has written the afterword for Building Worship Bridges.

music ministry, this is without a doubt the place to start (no question!).

**Why people attend this service.** It is very common to see worship services in churches that exist for the convenience of some staff and no one else. There is nothing wrong with groups of people getting together to worship privately in their own way. But that is not the same as hosting public worship.

**The fix:** Remove financial support. The group we described in our leader story is a big small group that is closed to new people. If you have a missional pastor, the best way to deal with that is to remove the pastor from the leadership of that service to start something that is truly missional. Let those that want that service form an experience of their own, but do not take up prime worship time on Sunday morning to do it. Work through appropriate decision making channels in your church to set the sequence of change; lead with the "why."

### Back to Tony Campolo

At the beginning of the chapter, we quoted Tony Campolo from an event at which Bishop Farr heard him speak. We do not know if Tony was promoting what some might call "blended worship." Some church growth consultants suggest that blending worship just winds up offending everyone. We do not necessarily agree. It always depends on what we blend and how we blend it. There are ways to juxtapose contemporary praise music and traditional hymns. The ancient-future style of worship is a blend that appeals to many different people in varied contexts. You may find recalcitrant choir directors and organists become more open to change using an ancient-future worship model. If that is the right model for your mission field, too, then by all means blend ancient and future together! (We introduced "ancient-future" in the workbook.)

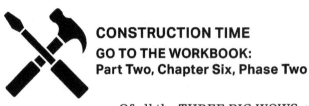

**CONSTRUCTION TIME**
**GO TO THE WORKBOOK:**
**Part Two, Chapter Six, Phase Two**

Of all the THREE BIG WOWS, music is the most demanding and the most difficult to change; it is also the most directly connected to the worship service per se. We will focus on music for the workbook portion of this chapter. We will show you how to improve the music in your church from where it is now, regardless of the style of your service (Spoken Liturgy or Live-Band-Led). In your workbook is a chart on how to juxtapose traditional and contemporary music in a single worship order that we might call *Ancient Future*. This chart will give you an inkling of where the worship order is headed in the chapters to come.

# Chapter Seven _____

## Phase Three: Technology

In 2015, the Walt Disney company released a new episode of the epic, multiple-decade-multiple-century-spanning story, Star Wars. One night, Cathy and her husband Terry tuned in to one of their favorite interviewers, Charlie Rose, to listen to him dialoguing with the originator of the series, George Lucas.

Lucas spoke about his use of technology to produce his blockbuster. He said, "You don't invent technology and then figure out what to do with it. You come up with an artistic problem and then you invent technology to accomplish it... Art of all levels is just technology." Lucas said, "I had a story to tell, there was a gap between what is possible and where my vision is, and I had to fill that gap (with technology)." [24]

Building a new steel-truss arch bridge that supports the traffic on the bridge is a very high tech endeavor. It is going to be the same for *Building Worship Bridges*. The church has a story to tell, too. Like Star Wars, we need technology to help us tell it. Our use of technology impacts how both old and new (to the church) experience the entire service, starting with the First Ten Minutes. The effect is negative when we are behind the technology curve. This shows up both in the quality and usage of the technology we already have and in our attitude about the need for using better and more diverse equipment. The church does not like to believe we need up-to-date technology to be the church. We do indeed need up-to-date technology when it comes to worship if we are a missionally focused churched. Technology is a supporting part of the worship journey, being part of the trusses! Here are some examples of the technology needed:

---

[24] Google "Charlie Rose Interview with George Lucas," or go to this web address: http://www.slashfilm.com/george-lucas-charlie-rose-interview/

- You need good equipment and someone who knows how to run it to make live music a WOW in the first ten minutes of your service. No one likes screeching and feedback while they are trying to focus their attention on God.

- Announcements belong in the Gathering time frame before the start of the Praise. (See the charts in the workbook for more information.) Embed them digitally into a looping video you create each week to scroll on the screen while the recorded background music is playing. Doing that involves at least three areas of technology: video, a screen, and background music. Some churches are still fighting over whether to have a screen let alone move announcements to appear on the screen.

- You can grow your service to about 75 attenders without a screen and without too many other upgrades. It is unusual for us to see churches with worship attendance over 75 that do not use a screen; but we have seen them, and even some as high as 150 or more. In churches without a screen that have attendance over 150, it is likely that the church once had much higher attendance but have now shrunk to 150. In those churches, we find that there is usually considerable conflict over worship and a lot of resistance to using the means of the day to reach new people. Churches that fight over worship and especially technology tend to have aging populations.

- As worship services grow, the need for technology increases because of the use of space and the impact of group dynamics upon that space. Technology upgrades always accompany church growth.

- Bishop Farr points out that while all generations have access to the same technology, we do not all use it in quite the same way. Technology is the great generational divide.

If you're about 60-ish, the PC was available to you in your mid to late 30's. But your toddler grandkids are conversant with their parents' smart phones or tablets often before they can walk or talk. Bishop Farr says it is not unusual to see five generations of worshippers in one setting (People live longer, thanks to technology!). Guess what divides these generations? We'll give you three tries, and the first two do not count.

## THE BIBLICAL THEME OF TECHNOLOGY:
### Energy for God's story

We bet you did not know that the Bible has a theme of technology. We did not either! We found out when we searched for it. We invite you to use the electronic genius Google to do the same. Search, "technology in the Bible." You will find several surprising passages that lead us to understand that the idea of technology in worship and church life is not new. Some of the passages support the use of technology to fulfill the purpose of being the church. Some warn us of becoming tied to technology and thus obscuring our purpose. You will hear both of those themes emerge in this chapter, too.

All parts of every worship service are important. In terms of first impressions and purpose, the Praise Segment (refer to the Workbook) is especially important. New people will often arrive late to your service. They will decide if they want to come back during your Praise Segment, not the Gathering. If your technology fails you then, you may have a problem removing obstacles. Additionally, the Praise Segment is about, well, praise.

It is a big part of God's story so we must tell it well. The Praise Segment in so many of our services is not a story; it is a plug and play. Excellent use of technology can help us boost the Praise Segment to give it energy so we tell God's story and ours with passion and purpose. But first we need to understand what Praise truly is and why it is so important.

## The purpose of The Praise Segment in the worship service

Praising is part of the missional worship experience – the gusset plate. Gusset plates provide structural stability for the trusses, which are the worship elements in our bridge metaphor. Without trusses and the supporting gusset plates, the road of the bridge would not be possible. In *Building Worship Bridges*, without the appropriate worship elements in a missional worship experience, there is no possibility for a worship journey.

The Praise Segment of the worship service is the time in the service when we sing songs of praise to and about God. During the time of Praise, we become part of the prophetic language of the Bible that every knee shall bow and every tongue confess that Jesus Christ is Lord. Public praise is a response to God's story and the way God's story intertwines with our own stories. It is a behavior that helps us both express and otherwise know (inside ourselves and our spirits) that we have something and someone to praise (Christ).

Which comes first? We again refer you to Google to find out. You will see a proliferation of verses about praising God in the Psalms among other books of the Bible. Why do you suppose God is telling us to spend so much time singing out loud to God? Consider this scripture:

> *The word that saves is right here, as near as the tongue in your mouth, as close as the heart in your chest. It's the word of faith that welcomes God to go to work and set things right for us. This is the core of our preaching. Say the welcoming word to God—"Jesus is my Master"— embracing, body and soul, God's work of doing in us what he did in raising Jesus from the dead.*
>
> **Romans 10:9-13, (MSG)**

This verse is not about praising God through singing per se. But it may indicate a sequence: declare with your mouth that Jesus is Lord and then believe in your heart. It is almost like step one and step two especially for someone new to Christianity and the life of the church. We confess during our singing of praise songs that Jesus is Lord. We may not say those words exactly, but we are singing to God or about God and that influences us all toward a mental belief in the reality of God. When we believe with our minds, God opens the doorway to believing with our hearts. Think of it this way:

*You had a fight with your spouse right before leaving for church and your spouse decided not to come with you. You come to church fuming and maybe a little depressed. Then you walk into a room and everyone around you is singing praises. Before long you have forgotten about your anger and self-pity. An hour later you go home with a certain level of forgiveness in your heart and have a conversation with your better half to work things out.*

Worshiping God pulls us out of ourselves for regulars and new people alike. In the public worship service, the dynamic of praise pulling us out of ourselves is a result of the words that come out of our mouths and the act of singing the praises that we are engaged in. Most experienced Christ followers and worshippers have a sense of this truth.

## TECHNICAL CONSTRUCTION

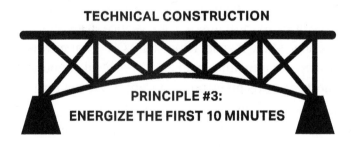

### PRINCIPLE #3:
### ENERGIZE THE FIRST 10 MINUTES

If it is true for church regulars (that praising God pulls us out of ourselves), it is also true for newcomers. Acts of singing and praise are the venue for worship. They are the venue for sharing God's story and our own. That is the sequence of worship that your hymnal lays out. The Praise time is right

101

after the Gathering and it is considered the start of your actual worship service. At least that is what we, the authors, endorse. Most services run an hour from The Praise through the time of dismissal. From this point forward, we will refer to The Praise as the start of your service in *Building Worship Bridges* and continue to encourage you to think of The Gathering as your pre-worship warm-up.

The start of the worship service is praise! Hallelujah! We are on the road to knowing God! Unfortunately, what we find in most worship services is a talking head at the start of the service. And that talking head is gabbing about announcements. The announcements are usually all about trying to get sign-ups for what are often ministries that are not gaining traction in church life.

If anything says to your guest, "this church is all about us and you do not really belong," it is talking head announcements. How did the church get so far afield from creating an environment of praise with taking advantage of a captive audience to keep the machine alive?

Singing songs of praise is a way for new people to see the faith community believing in God. Your Praise Segment should be a WOW of music and hospitality. The energy you give it will impact the next fifty minutes of your service in either a good or bad direction. Make it good; make it a WOW. That means finding another place for announcements. Talking head announcements will almost certainly guarantee your guest will not return.

Announcements drone on and steal the vibrancy that the Praise Segment should instill. Often the announcements also include inside language that multiples the disconnect for the guest. The service never recovers. For you to be able to eliminate announcements from the Praise

Segment of your service requires that we return to the main topic of this chapter: technology.

**PREPARE YOUR CHURCH FOR GUESTS:** *Interactive*

In so many of our churches, The Praise Segment is detached when it should be interactive. Praising God is by nature interactive between God and persons in seats as well as persons in seats with one another. When the energy in the room is low ...

- because the music is lifeless and/or
- because we do not have a screen and/or
- because the sound equipment is dated and/or
- because we have just experienced talking head
- announcements and/or
- because worship leaders do not know how to lead worship in a way that connects with guests

... the worship's vibrancy has been stolen right out from under our noses. Additionally, the experience is not only not culturally normal, but it also does not allow us to fulfill the purpose of the time of public praise in the worship gathering. Remind yourself of your recent trip to see your home team play ball:

*While you were smooching with your honey, a hidden telephoto lens found you and voilà! You were on the Jumbotron. Your friends followed stats on the electronic scoreboard and players on Twitter. You logged on to "like" the sports arena on your way to hanging out in the open-air bar to mingle with other imbibers while glancing at the flat screen with the game on it.*

Who goes to a baseball game anymore just to watch the game? Who goes to a worship service any more just to be an object in seats? Think of every person in seats as a worship producer [26] lest we quickly lose their attention as they wonder why we are doing worship to them instead of with them.

Again, we share a caveat: none of what we are suggesting to you is truly about the technology. As integral as technology is, the ability to use it well comes from the deeper reality of why we are doing this work in the first place.

We must be all-in to want to reach new people. We must also be all-in to give both new and regulars a place to land and a reason to come back. If the only thing people experience in your church is great technology, there is no reason for them to return.

Everything we are discussing reflects the original premise that we are developing relationships with the mission field. Without relationships, we are still just a talking head. We footnoted the PEW study on church attendance in Part One. The reason churches grow is because of discipleship, not because of high-tech.

If you can use technology to help you tell the story people long to hear with their hearts to lead them to be Christ followers, you will gain traction.

### THE GUEST EXPERIENCE: *Engaged*

In our guest story, our guest is late getting to her seat in the worship space. As she acclimates to her surroundings, she is drawn into the experience by several factors. See if you can identify those before getting to the debrief.

### A guest's experience

*When you made your way into the worship space at Accelerating Church, you weren't sure just how late you were. They finished the music and the person got up to talk. You wondered if you were going to hear a bunch of announcements like you did at Decelerating Church. That didn't happen. Yay! The chick up there seemed cool.*

---

[26] The Growing Technological Generation Gap, Feb 12, 2013; http://theindustry. cc/2013/02/12/the-growing-technological-generation-gap/

*Anyway, you did find your thoughts going back to when the guy at Decelerating Church said, "We are so glad you're here." You wondered who "we" was. You figured it wasn't you. You really felt like an outsider. You were kind of glad he said it because it made it easier for you to get up and leave. You hesitated even though you practically already had one foot out the door. And then they started all those announcements. You're outta there.*

*Accelerating Church felt pretty normal. Lots of people in the room were singing. The music was like the quality of a recording. Some people were kind of just watching and listening, but that seemed okay. At one point the worship leader said something about how cool it was to see everyone participating in different ways. That made you think. There was a lot going on in that room. The screens had movement; that was different than Decelerating Church. That screen back there looked super old fashioned. These at Accelerating Church were like at a football game. Even though you weren't sing-ing much, those screens  made it seem pretty easy to get involved while you were just watching.*

*When that chick got up to talk, she said her two-year-old decided to have a tantrum on his way there with her this morning. She said her son made her late and frazzled, but then some people prayed with her when she got there and she settled down. You remembered those days when your kids were little. You wondered if she had a husband. She didn't mention anyone. She wasn't up there very long, but long enough to invite people to meet up with her at the coffee bar after the service. She talked about a 5K run to raise money for the food shelf; she looked like a runner. Maybe you could bring your kids with you on the run; you ran with them a lot. It would be good for them to get involved in something that was for someone else.*

*The chick prayed with people in the service when she was done. It was like every day talk from her heart. You remembered back to the prayers you said in church when you were a kid growing up. You had to read them. It was weird. You couldn't connect to any of the words. And then when the pastor said a prayer, well ... it was lots of words.*

105

*Right after she finished a video started playing. You felt emotional and you hoped you didn't start crying right there in front of everyone. It wasn't too bad right now because the lighting was low enough to cover your face. That chick had talked about the prayer chapel and you thought about going there. Maybe next time.*

*As you got up to go, you saw a reminder to go visit that welcomer chick at the coffee bar, with her picture on the screen. You got your kids and then went over.*

## GUEST EXPERIENCE DEBRIEF: *From Praise to Interest*

The first thing we notice is that our guest arrived late yet she felt more comfortable here than at *Decelerating Church* where she was on time. Lighting may have been part of that.

Perhaps it was also the attitude that *Accelerating Church* projected through their upfront leadership and words that

*Decelerating Church* did not: a desire to connect. Let's now take a look at what was helpful for *Building Worship Bridges*:

**We are so glad you're here.** Our guest heard that phrase at *Decelerating Church*. We hear that phrase a lot too. It often comes off rote, formulaic, and inauthentic. Churches say it because they want to welcome people, but the phrasing itself creates a barrier between insiders and outsiders.

> **The fix:** Use "I" language. If you are an upfront leader with an opportunity to speak to the congregation to welcome the congregation verbally, say something like, "I am so grateful to be in worship with everyone here today."
> Additionally, you can suggest that everyone that is there is a worship leader. See the chart on increasing participation in the workbook companion chapter.

**Getting there late.** If a guest arrives right on time or late to your service, they should find a strong musical start to your service.

Do not greet them with announcements!

**The fix:** Understand announcements are JUST FOR US. JUST FOR US activities are focused on church people and occur usually in the church building or meeting place. They include things like the pancake breakfast, the cleaning up of the church basement, a pot luck meal, a Bible study, a choir practice, and a board meeting, to name a few things we normally see in traditional church life. The announcement for each activity is in the scrolling, looping video we spoke about above.

Announcements looping before the service give persons in seats a window into community life. These do not yield many sign-ups; but neither do the verbal announcements we make to strong arm participation in what are often dying ministries in our churches. Regular attenders do not all have a sense of duty to rescue an upcoming event from languishing due to lack of attention or interest. And new people won't attend what only regulars attend. They do not know you well enough yet. When a ministry is engaging, sign-ups for it will come in two ways: through our use of electronic / social media, and personal invitation. If you cannot get people to come to a JUST FOR US activity through social media and personal invitation, it is probably time to end the activity.

**Welcome and Invitation.** The guest was interested in the up-front welcomer (that "chick!") because she connected to her. Her personal connection opened her ears to the connecting points the upfront leader mentioned that were coming up during the week.

**The fix:** Understand the Welcome and Invitation is JUST FOR THEM. If your style is spoken-liturgy, the praise section should begin with a hymn or two. If it is live-band-led, it will probably start with three songs. In both cases, the Praise section ends with a welcome. Look at the companion chapter in the workbook section to learn how to put together a great welcome.

During the welcome, the welcome host invites persons in seats to JUST FOR THEM activities which usually take place outside the church building. JUST FOR THEM events and activities are missional, helping us reach out to people that are not part of our faith communities. These activities would be anything the church does to be the church in the world (i.e. serving a meal at the homeless shelter).

Missional invitations can also include things that tie the worship service to discipleship (i.e. an invitation to the start of a new small group). [28] Sign-ups for JUST FOR THEM events increase when persons in seats receive a personal invitation from the host to connect personally with the host after the service (in addition to the social media advertising and sign up opportunities). Look to the workbook for some charts in the corresponding workbook chapter on How to Create a Strong Welcome for Guests.

**A personal connection.** In our story, the guest connected spiritually with the woman who did the welcome and invitation because the she gave a snippet of a personal testimony. Peer connections are very important in helping people return.

**The fix:** Develop lay hosts! Select hosts carefully. They must be growing in faith, have the respect of their peers, represent the mission field, and have the skill set and gifts of public presentation. Cathy can attest to the power of peer influence. She and her husband went to church for the first time in a

---

[28] We distinguish between new groups and existing groups because new people will more likely get involved in a group that is just starting than in one that has been around a while.

long time during a rough spot early in their marriage. At that service, a woman about Cathy's age shared some things about her involvement in ministry. Cathy turned to her husband and said, "I'd like to do that." It was the start of a complete life change for Cathy and her family. P.S. You will need to develop a training system for raising up hosts.

**Different forms of participation.** The role of the worship leader is to usher persons in seats into the presence of Christ during the worship service. We cast the vision for participation by identifying various options for how to participate.

> **The fix:** Vision casting. The worship leader helps persons in seats interact. They do this by communicating that all of us are worship leaders when we worship God through watching, thinking, observing, considering, singing praises, weeping, and hoping.

**The Sound System and Screen Usage.** Nothing distracted the guest at *Accelerating Church* in our chapter story. If people notice your technology, it usually means something is wrong with it, or with the way you are using it.

> **The fix:** Updating and upgrading your sound system, getting a screen, and learning how to utilize your equipment well. See the workbook for a chart on how to use a screen.

We've been talking about a projection screen. We must also mention flat screens. They are as important for the church as they are in people's homes. *Accelerating Church* has them in various areas of their lobby (you might not see any bulletin boards at *Accelerating Church*). You will see small gatherings of people sitting in chairs surrounding the screen watching the service as they interact with one another and perhaps nurse babies or comfort wiggly toddlers.

If your church is under 75 in worship attendance or if you do not have a screen, get a 60" flat screen on a mobile stand and hook your laptop and Wi-Fi to it. Bishop Farr knows of a church of about 20 in worship that has done this to feature choirs and other music for their small numbers of persons in seats to sing along with. The cost is surprisingly low.

**Videos.** Videos are a fantastic communication tool that you cannot use if you do not have some type of screen. Work on getting a screen to accommodate video production.

**The fix:** Buy a subscription (after you get a screen). Videos abound for scripture, preaching themes, and other segues or countdowns. Buy a package to keep costs down. Make your own videos using your cell phone to show congregational life. Keep them under two minutes.

### ADAPTIVE CONSTRUCTION

PRINCIPLE #3:
ENERGIZE SPIRITUAL PRACTICES

*"Who dares despise the day of small things, since the seven eyes of the LORD that range throughout the earth will rejoice when they see the chosen capstone in the hand of Zerubbabel?"*

**Zechariah 4:10 (MSG)**

We are not called to create the best worship service on the face of the earth out of our own willpower. Creating missional worship is a gusset plate of stability, providing support to the trusses (the elements of worship). But without the piers (missional focus) for the trusses (worship elements) and gusset plates (the missional worship service) to attach to, there would be no bridge (connection between the church and the neighbor-hood) and no road (the worship journey). In other words, without discipleship, it is nearly impossible for an upfront worship leader to lead authentically. Anything less than a fully devoted spiritual life on the worship road with God leaves a worship service superficial and wanting.

The worship journey requires discipline. Leaders of all stripes often get caught up in the busyness of leadership. When tasks distract us, we find ourselves making our decisions in the flesh, not in concert with what God is asking of us or leading us toward. Most of us will only have time for God when we organize ourselves to take that time. Or maybe taking the time for God will force us to organize the rest of our lives better and with more discipline.

Either way, if we are just too busy to take the time for God, it will show up in our upfront leadership. Look to the following two organizational practices to give you more time for spiritual down-time with God:

**Develop teams.** We must hand off to others a lot of the work we are doing ourselves to free us up to stay connected to God.

**Trust down time.** The work of worship happens as much during the week as it does in the one hour we have for it on a Sunday morning. Remember, the worship journey is 24/7.

### PREPARE YOURSELF FOR GUESTS: *Daily Devotions*

Team development grows your church organizationally and spiritually. Team development is an adaptive skill that time with God enables. We do not get very far as public leaders in raising up more leaders without our own personal, daily devotional time with God in a way that is disciplined and open to God's pruning as we study.

Leaders that waffle when there is pushback have trouble giving away leadership to others and asking a lot of volunteers. Without time alone with God, leaders can get harsh with people they might need to correct through spiritual and relational authority. Or they might avoid correction altogether. Younger leaders will hesitate to ask more of older parishioners because the younger leader does not trust their own leadership role that God has called them to.[29]

Insecure public leaders make excuses for bad behavior among parishioners instead of having a loving but firm come-to-Jesus conversation about community life. If we are driven by recognition of our own talent among the laity, we will often spend all our time doing and none of our time being.

Almost always, we, the authors, can find a direct link between leadership weakness and the daily devotional time with God that challenges us to think more deeply about how to be a leader. We only grow when we practice our calling to live out our calling. Olympic Gold medal platform diver Tom Daley put it this way:

*"I think the real reason for my improvement is because I had such a long period in the off-season just working as hard as I could ..."* [30]

Worship leaders must learn to live in the off season, too: the six days a week between services. Those are the small times in which we might not see much action, especially if we are seeking after God and learning to lead in new ways. We want the change to happen quickly but adaptive change happens more slowly. We need to trust that the small times are the times that will most impact what we do on Sunday mornings because we will not always see immediate results.

---

[29] We recommend Rob Bell's book How to Be Here, a very current style book on spiritual practices. In that book, Rob calls us human beings, not human doings. We like that!

[30] Tom Daley, Olympic Gold Medal Diver, http://www.brainyquote.com/quotes/quotes/t/tomdaley426396.html?src=t_repetition

Living into our upfront worship leadership role is a worship journey process of digging deep. That is why we need the mid-week connection with God.

## A leader's experience

*Maybe it was that a guest showed up unexpectedly and then left before the service even got started that made you do it. Maybe it was all those thoughts that went through your head about how the people that attended your service were going through the motions. Maybe it was thinking about how you were kind of cold and distant to your band.*

*Maybe it was the new pastor that came to the church and her conversations with you about making this service more relevant and engaging. God seemed to have a wicked sense of humor. Timing is everything. You were considering quitting and now someone was suggesting you needed to do better in your work. With all your inner thoughts God seemed to have already opened the doorway to you receiving that kind of critique from the new pastor. It was hard to hear when the pastor and you had that come-to-Jesus meeting, still, you heard it. She was giving you some time to decide what you wanted to do.*

*So, you found yourself on your knees. You heard yourself begging God. "God, help me connect my life together. Get me out of this downward spiral. Help me recognize the calling you have for me. Show me how to lead." You heard yourself begging God for connection inside yourself frequently, throughout the days and nights, using the same words over and over and over.*

*It seemed like God heard you. After about a week of your new-found, soul-searching behavior, the new pastor suggested you take a weekend off and take your band with you to Accelerating Church. She said she would do some other things to cover the music. She asked you if you had ever attended Accelerating Church. The truth was you hadn't. You had only listened to their recorded music. She was right, you thought; you needed to see for yourself. You decided that the new pastor must basically think you had something to offer if she was asking you to step up to the plate. Deal. You were in. You set it up with your band. A month later, you went to Accelerating Church. It was an eye opener for you and the musicians.*

*They were really good at Accelerating Church. But more than that, they were nice. You felt really welcomed. Someone who introduced themselves to you asked you what brought you here. When you told him who you were, he asked if you wanted to meet the worship leader. You said sure, so the greeter said to meet him at the coffee bar after the service and he'd introduce you. You showed up there and so did the greeter. When you met the worship leader, he told you he'd be very happy to help you rebuild your service. That was the most incredible thing.*

**LEADER EXPERIENCE DEBRIEF:** *Growing Stronger*

We, the authors, can tell you about different times in our spiritual leadership when we were on our knees with weeping and gnashing of teeth. The only way we made it through trying times was through our own surrender. Let's now take a look at what was revealed in our leader's story:

**Begging God.** If you have ever struggled with your personal life and your leadership life being at odds, then you may know what it is like to beg God for mercy. If you do not know what it is like to beg God for mercy, may we suggest you give it a try.

> **The fix:** Deep travailing. Our prayer lives are incredibly important to our ability to lead others. "Travailing" is a place of prayer inside where there are no words, only moanings and groanings of the Spirit. God understands those. To lead with strength and power, go to that place, ask God to be in that leadership with you, to remove obstacles, and to show

you the way forward.

**Being a recipient of a "come-to-Jesus" talk.** If you are paid or non-paid staff and your leader asks you to raise the bar on your leadership performance, how will you respond?

> **The fix:** Respond with gratitude. Our spiritually-growing worship leader had a new thought that he might be someone the new pastor wanted to keep around. That's how we should respond to correction from spiritual authorities in our lives. Return to deep travailing.

**Leadership skills.** The new pastor was not afraid to ask for more. You do not have to be a brand-new leader in a new environment to develop those leadership chops.

> **The fix:** See yourself as a growing leader. Return to deep travailing to ask God to give you the skills.

**Field trip.** If you have not been to *Accelerating Church*, then take some time to go.

> **The fix:** Scheduling. Worship leaders of all stripes should get out of their own church to see what is going on in nearby growing churches.

**CONSTRUCTION TIME**
**GO TO THE WORKBOOK,**
**Part Two, Chapter Seven, Phase Three**

The discussion of technology in the first part of this chapter causes us to think about other parts of the worship service that require technology, too. We are better prepared for ramping up with high tech when we are grounded spiritually. We have taken the time to temper the grind toward updating and upgrading technology by addressing spiritual leadership in the discussion about the Praise Segment of your service.

Technology moves so fast that by the time this book is published, our ideas may be obsolete! Do keep pushing forward from that spiritual place in you, not the technical place. If technology fails, you will still have your relationship with God to share with others. Head to the workbook to learn now about numerous ways technology will help you tell God's story.

# Chapter Eight _____

## Phase Four: Discipleship

If you are serious about *Building Worship Bridges*, there is a
worship design team in your future. If you are a smaller church,
you may be thinking it is a mere fantasy to dream of a worship
design team. Or you may be wondering what a worship design
team is. Even larger churches often do not have much experience with worship design teams. Whether your faith community
is larger or smaller, you may be wondering about the connection between a design team and discipleship. Let's see if we can
answer some of those questions and concerns.

A pastor Kay was working with had never worked with a
worship design team before. He was a lone ranger and perfectly
content in being so. When Kay suggested he assemble a design
team, he was hesitant but eventually reluctantly agreed to
proceed. When the team was assembled, Kay met with them for
the first time. The group was talented no doubt, but had never
tapped into their collective creativity to create a worship experience. This was a new journey for them to say the least. When
Kay suggested we begin with prayer, they easily agreed.

However, her second request was a bit more challenging for
the team. "Let us all share our "God moments." Kay explained ×
we would be sharing where God is working in our lives in the
past few weeks. This team, the very group leading worship, was
uncomfortable sharing where God was intersecting in their lives
with one another. How could they share God with the congregation if they were not comfortable sharing it with one another?
The team seemed further confused by the fact that they had been
assembled to "design worship" not talk about God! Oh, what a
disconnect! Unfortunately, this is not an uncommon occurrence.

As this worship design team began to trust and grow in rela-

117

tionship with one another, they found sharing God moments to come easier and easier. This led to being more comfortable in sharing their stories during worship. The more time they spent sharing their own stories and digging deep into understanding the hopes, concerns, and fears of those attending worship, the more relevant the worship was for those attending (that's cool). As the team began to dig deeper into understanding who the unchurched were in their mission field, the more they could shift the worship experience to fit.

Because of their personal growth in discipleship, the team could share both the church's stories as well as their own personal stories. This allowed the team to be relatable to attenders which led to a much more vibrant, relevant, and compelling worship experience.

## THE BIBLICAL THEME OF DISCIPLESHIP: *Paying it Forward* *(The Great Commission and the Great Commandment)*

In Chapter One, we introduced the theme of God's Biblical story of worship and the sub theme of salvation. We identified that worshiping God transforms us as God teaches us to love ourselves the way God loves us. The more comfortable we grow in our own skin, the more fully human we are. Worship and the resulting new identity in Christ is our destiny. God created us for that purpose. God's story and our stories intertwine.

We recognize this growing, Godly relationship as discipleship. Worship is our overarching relationship with God; discipleship is how we live out the worship relationship in community. The worship design team you read about in Kay's opening story is an example of how the church lives out the discipleship value (the pier of *Building Worship Bridges*) as a part of the structure of church life. Individuals with specific gifts grow as disciples within their area of giftedness (creative types!) as they participate on that team.

Team participants also "pay it forward;" they share with

others what they know about God and impact the body through their work. As disciples, we are all called to live out our faith to grow stronger as disciples and to pay it forward to others. Our worship relationship with God implies we must do both (the Great Commission). Our Christian identity implies we will lose our own soul if we do not do both (the Great Commandment).

Discipleship is the pier sitting on the footing of our worship bridge. Discipleship is the very fundamental undergirding of the missional focus (the footing). The value of discipleship must play out in behavior. Therefore, intentional discipling (the pier) is part of the missional worship (the gusset plate) focus that allows access into and out of church life through the worship journey (the road). *Building Worship Bridges* facilitates discipleship connections:

> *¹ So, my son, throw yourself into this work for Christ. ² Pass on what you heard from me - the whole congregation saying Amen! - to reliable leaders who are competent to teach others.*
>
> **2 Timothy 2:1-2 (MSG)**

Our passage suggests that we need mature Christians, alongside less mature Christians for the value of discipleship to show up behaviorally. We call that a discipleship system. We did not write this book to help you put a discipleship system together. Kay has written other resources for that (AKA, "intentional faith development processes"). [31] It is a major undertaking for a church, thus it is a separate topic.

In *Building Worship Bridges*, we call attention to the intentionality of a discipleship process. Your worship design team is a part of the faith formation process you already have or will put in place. We will get to the process (with significant detail) of working with a design team in our workbook companion chapter. We want to keep our current focus on the impact of discipleship as a value and a behavior in overall worship design.

---

[31] Gear Up by Kotan, Abingdon Press 2017

**Starting with the end in mind**

Discipleship and worship go hand in hand. Therefore, we must see the influence of worship in discipleship and discipleship in worship. In the worship service, the influence of discipleship will most affect the ending of the service which must be strong to complement the beginning. In many of our churches, the ending is weak. Every church needs places to invite people to after the service. People walking out your door need a hand off – a "what's next?"

It might be participation in a small group, missional outreach, participation in a work area of church life, or something we have not mentioned. It might be as simple as invite a friend to join you next week, or tell someone about how you experienced God today. If the only thing a person ever did after a worship service was to tell someone else about Jesus, did that church fulfill its purpose? We think so! Discipleship might be as much about who we become as what we do.

Improving your worship service ending is the next action in your order of change. Start with the end in mind to develop the worship service and thread the end of the service into the beginning of the service for discipleship to take root in worship design.

## TECHNICAL CONSTRUCTION

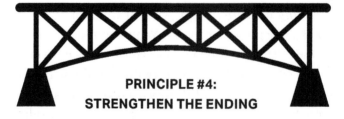

**PRINCIPLE #4:**
**STRENGTHEN THE ENDING**

In most of the worship services we experience, the ending goes like this:

- pastor ends the sermon
- some rote prayers and rituals
- song, benediction, and that's all folks!

For a person that took the time to attend your service, the lack of attention to "what is next" leaves a gaping hole. Think of the seeker who has a God-sized hole they are looking to fill only to leave with a gaping hole! A new person may have already decided to return because of front end hospitality. But if there is no attention to what is next in a prominent way at the end of your service (and if the new person wants to grow) she will not likely stick around over time. Discipleship sticks, like an Olympic vault landing. [32]

But the real key to threading discipleship into the worship service is to start the invitation process early (as early as the welcome) which occurs about ten minutes into the service. This is right after the Praise Segment, and right before the Proclamation in the workbook. Remember: discipleship really starts even before the welcome, and before the Gathering Segment of your worship service. It starts as early as your website when it is used as a discipling tool.

Back to the worship service. Every week, the welcome should include something that encourages both guests and regulars to mingle after the worship service, to do something of value missionally during the week, and to think about why they should come back next week to experience community life during public worship. Not everyone will take you up on your offer, but if you do not offer for sure very few new people will stick. Guests make up their minds about returning to your church in large part because of your hospitality efforts during the Gathering or the Praise. A strong ending can solidify their decision or help them speed up their return. *Accelerating Church* understands we are

---

[32] Six Reasons Congregations Have Become Sticky, Ibid

only a first-time guest one time (on the road into the church on the worship bridge). The missionally focused church (on the road out to the community on the worship bridge) intertwines and promotes discipleship. That is the way they bring new people back across the bridge.

We have said that the ending of your service begins during the welcome. But it begins during the Praise when some people are making up their minds about returning. The Praise segment should be powerful for anyone to even consider paying attention to what you say in the Welcome and then to whatever happens after that. Everything in your service affects the next thing in the service. When the Praise Segment is strong, then the

Welcome facilitates the transition to the Proclamation (scripture reading, sermon, and all videos or other artistic endeavors associated with the sermon).Disciples need to hear the Word of God spoken powerfully. The welcome time that is a transition indicates we are about to go deeper in the worship experience, so "stay tuned." The Response comes after the sermon (prayers, tithes, offerings, communion, or other interactive worship practices). In the worship orders, we have laid out for you, the Response deepens the sermon even more. Now we are getting somewhere! Finally, the Dismissal (closing hymn, benediction and exit) is a clue it is time to put it all into practice.

## PREPARE YOUR CHURCH FOR GUESTS: *Relationships*

In worship design, we are constantly thinking about how people connect to God and each other during the worship service, especially new people. The focus on new people is encouraging to regulars, too, if regulars are growing disciples who long to give Jesus away to new people. Discipleship is relational and so is worship. We will disciple new people and church regulars through an intentional missional focus and invitation during the worship service when we:

**Tie this week's service to next week's service.**

We are not talking about your sermon series or the trendy guest speaker you're so pumped about that's, "... gonna knock everyone's socks off." We hear that type of language a lot. It is formulaic, if not contrived. It has the opposite effect you desire if someone is looking for authenticity. Go ahead and mention the new sermon series, but do it in a way that is personal and revealing something about yourself along the way. Here is an example: for a host to say: *I am personally interested in the new sermon series about Why Bad Things Happen to Good People because my father's sister's son—that would be my cousin—just got in a big jam in his life that has been so hard for my aunt to deal with. So, if you want to come next week, meet me at the coffee bar after worship today and we'll talk about where we sit next week. We can go for coffee after and talk about it.*

Now that's an invitation! Persons in seats need to grasp that something is happening on-site at your church that doesn't happen anywhere else, such as:

- Powerful, live praise
- Personal connections with up front leaders
- Persons in seats connecting with each other after the service

These things cannot happen if you stay home.

**Tie today's experience to the "real world."**

A transformational experience for a person in seats is transferable to another person in that worshiper's life if it is culturally relevant to the person that is worshiping with you. Discipleship always occurs in the context of everyday life. Many people – old and new alike – are looking for reasons to invite people they care about to the worship service, where things happen "live" that do not happen anywhere else. We help all persons in seats reach out to their friends through discipleship threads and cultural relevance in our services. Missionally focused churches also provide an invitation tool for attenders. Missionally focused worship (the gusset plate) provides a worship journey (the roadway) that provides two-way traffic across the worship bridge.

**Tie the end of today's service to the beginning of today's service.**

Worshipers must know what is happening within the single hour in which they are present in your service to be able to draw a connection between their own life, God and community life. How are you guiding people through the service from beginning to end to help the service make sense? How are we providing a connectional thread throughout the entire worship experience? When things make sense, discipleship deepens a little more, and we gain confidence that we can invite our friends into the experience and they will connect, too.

Now work your way back up the list we just provided. We represent the beginning of your service in the last sub heading above. All the way back up to the beginning of our list (two more sub headings) takes you to the end of the service. We are beginning with the end in mind.

The host brings all attenders' attention to these dynamics during the Welcome. We reinforce the words the host uses with a strong discipleship system that we have developed behind the scenes. Now we are ready for our guest.

**THE GUEST EXPERIENCE:** *Connecting the dots*

Let's eavesdrop on the guest's thoughts as the guest is listening to the host welcome the congregation. Notice the many threads of connection that help the guest connect her own life to church life during the invitational welcome, and then after the service, too.

### A guest's experience

*One of the things that you thought sounded cool at Accelerating Church was when they talked about how a few of the study groups and relationship groups were going to the homeless shelter to serve a meal this week. You didn't know what a relationship group was, but you figured it was people hanging out. You wondered about a study group and if you'd fit in with one. The chick up front said some of the groups were doing a fasting covenant (or agreement) together. You never used the word "covenant" in your life (you were pretty sure), but you understood fasting from dieting. You thought about how you'd like to fast from partying for a while. You wondered if you would. The host said you could go to the coffee bar after the service to find out more about the homeless shelter and the groups. She said to talk to this guy who would be there and then she put his picture on the screen. You decided to stop there. You thought it might be nice for your kids to go to a homeless shelter, just in case they wondered if they had it good or not. The welcomer said that next Sunday they were going to talk about fasting in church during the sermon. You wanted to be here for that.*

### GUEST EXPERIENCE DEBRIEF: *Inklings of Discipleship*

There is a lot going on in our story, even though it is short. We hope you picked up on all the elements. If not, here is a recap of the major points for learning.

**Groups.** The growth of your service depends in large part upon the development of some type of relational group. Groups are also the opportunity for diving into discipleship growth opportunities. But typically, a connection through relationships comes before beginning discipleship. Resources abound on line and through other churches.

**The fix:** Find language for your groups. Some might suggest using the language "small groups." That is not as guest friendly in the 21st Century as it was in the 80's and 90's. Many churches have come up with a name for such groups that suits their context. Examples are life groups or growth ✓ groups. Find your group identity, then follow a process for developing facilitators and multiplying groups.

**Fasting and covenants.** Many mainliners do not know what fasting is since the only time mainliners fast is during Lent. When you use church language, be prepared to explain it. Your newcomers will like it and your regulars will learn a few things, too.

**The fix:** Increase the use of spiritual practices all year long. Spiritual practices (or disciplines) are a way for new people to grow in their faith and for church regulars to increase their faith. Including spiritual practices in the worship service that you have practiced during the week deepens the worship experience. More on this topic in the Workbook.

**What actually touches people.** The guest was interested in fasting because she had experienced it dieting. She wondered about how it might apply to partying.

**The fix:** Communicate. We are creating threads of discipleship in the worship service when we guide the thinking of persons in seats to grasp what we are trying to teach them. Talking about fasting during the welcome did not take long and it accomplished the goal of drawing in the guest and tying this week's service to next.

**The coffee bar and pictures on the screen.** Creating a coffee bar ✓ is a good way to invite people to stick around after the service and find out more about your church. The coffee bar creates a specific connecting point. Using pictures during your invite creates connections, interest and ease in connecting. This is part of the hospitality truss in our overall worship bridge design.

**The fix:** It's not about the coffee or the coffee bar. We shared this truth once already. It is important so we are sharing it again. Remember, the bar creates the opportunity for a connection and/or relationship building.

**Reinforcing the decision.** The guest may have made up her mind to come back during the Praise or when the connector took her to the kids' area and back and served her coffee. Regardless, she reinforced her decision to stick around when she started thinking about involving her kids in going to a homeless shelter.

**The fix:** Create a strong invitation that leads to a strong ending.

**ADAPTIVE CONSTRUCTION**

**PRINCIPLE #4:**
**STRENGTHEN THE DESIGN PROCESS**

*I planted the seed, Apollos watered the plants, but God made you grow. It's not the one who plants or the one who waters who is at the center of this process but God, who makes things grow. Planting and watering are menial servant jobs at minimum wages. What makes them worth doing is the God we are serving. You happen to be God's field in which we are working.*

**1 Corinthians 3: 6-9 (MSG)**

Google, "teamwork in the Bible" to find numerous passages on God's design for how we work together to be the Body of Christ. Teamwork is part of God's creativity. Let that be your motivation to develop the workgroups associated with worship design. You will need many teams to build your worship bridge, including the following:

- The band and worship leading teams.
- Hospitality teams.
- Children's ministry teams.
- Prayer team.
- Small group development team.
- Discipleship team.

Each team will need a coordinator to recruit people to that team, then organize, train and deploy team members to various jobs in their work areas. Two other teams form the remaining focus of the rest of this chapter and our workbook: the worship design and sermon writing teams. The pastor is typically the primary leader of these teams because worship design and sermon development is so very important in *Building Worship Bridges*. We will not expound on how team development works here.

## PREPARE YOURSELF FOR GUESTS: *An Unoffendable Spirit*

We selected the Bible verse at the beginning of this section out of all other numerous options because of the variation of jobs: some plant, some water but God makes you grow and gets the glory! Creative people tend to want recognition.

Successful worship design and sermon writing teams are comprised of creative persons who can handle not always getting the glory. It is called humility! For most creative types, having humility where their work is concerned is a significant learning curve.

The most profound learning curve of working with a design team is developing an unoffendable spirit. The epitome of maturity in Christian discipleship is holding everything loosely and not rushing to judgment and anger when something does not go your way. Christ followers are unoffendable because we trust in the power of confession and forgiveness through our Lord Jesus Christ. Creative design teams are awesome because they can communicate Christian truths in unusual and clever ways. But creative design teams are powerful when Christian themes of trust and transformation come through their design work with authenticity.

Many pastors are creative types. They can be the hardest ones to coach! They are busy and they trust their own creativity, so they pull videos, dramas and music together very quickly, and often alone. What they lose in doing so is raising up more leaders and setting the tone for holding work loosely. The creativity that comes through working with a team is important. It is also secondary to the investment that any leader makes in developing more disciples in their midst (by working together to develop worship). Pastors that have learned to let go of their ego in worship design can guide the rest of the team to do that, too. A favorite blogger put it this way:

*If your work has never been criticized, it's unlikely you have any work. Creating work is the point, though, which means that in order to do something that matters, you're going to be criticized. If your goal is to be universally liked and respected and understood, then, it must mean your goal is not to do something that matters. Which requires hiding. Hiding, of course, isn't the point. Hence the paradox. You don't want to be criticized and you do want to matter. The solution: Create work that gets criticized. AND, have the discernment to tell the difference between useful criticism (rare and precious) and the stuff worth ignoring (everything else).* [33]

We should all want our work to be critiqued with care and an eye toward reflecting spiritual maturity. Churches grow because

---

[33] Seth Godin, The Paradox of the Flawless Record; http://sethgodin.typepad.com/seths_blog/2016/09/the-paradox-of-the-flawless-record.html

of innovation and because of discipleship. In the worship design and sermon writing teams, innovation and discipleship dovetail. Worship design grows strong through intentional creativity in the face of reality and truth telling – behind the scenes work that readies you for guests.

## THE LEADER EXPERIENCE: *Evaluation*

Evaluation takes different forms. Sometimes it is formal like with the worship design team who develop systems for weekly evaluation. Some evaluation occurs in conversations when persons in seats tell you about their response to your work. Some of what they say can be valuable while some is just noise. Learn the difference. The type of evaluation that most matters is self-evaluation. In the previous chapter's leader story, the leader began to see things about himself that needed to change. Let's see how self-evaluation makes its way into team development, and ultimately into the worship service. We pick up our protagonist's story six months from the last one.

### A leader's experience

*It had been an interesting six months since you had that come-to-Jesus meeting with the new pastor. You liked her and you also struggled with her. She was asking a lot of you and she was not necessarily giving you many complements to let you know how good your work is. You found yourself mouthing off to her at times. Amazingly, she took it. She had a lot of self-assurance, you thought, and focus. She wanted to get somewhere with the church and with new people. She was very serious about her work and apparently about your work, too! All the while, you found your work improving. You smirked and chuckled as you thought about that.*

*Shutting down the service you had been leading was not easy. You thought the new pastor handled it great, but still, people were mad. Some left. Some got over it. Some stayed and kept carrying on. Some of the naysayers were in the band. With the new pastor's help, you had your own "come-to-Jesus" meetings with them and found yourself feeling pretty good about how you handled it. Six months ago, it would have been a very different experience. But now, even former band members and singers that didn't want to do things a new way seemed to be over their bitterness. You were over yours, too, which helped you help them. As to the others, well, you had to let them go.*

*Starting over again with the service was a completely different experience than the last time you started your service. You could see why things didn't work out before. You found yourself thinking back to that day the Guest came and left. You knew she was the kind of person you'd want to come to your new service. You knew that if you had ever had a chance to interact with someone like her now, it might lead to that person getting pretty involved in what you were doing.*

*You had heard the story of the woman who greeted the Guest in the lobby that day. That woman had told everyone about how that Guest was never going to be able to raise her kids right. That woman was no longer involved in greeting! That was a good thing. You also thought a lot about all those rantings you had with God for a while. Apparently, God heard you every time you begged God to give you direction. You were grateful.*

## LEADER EXPERIENCE DEBRIEF: *Transformational Mentoring*

The transformation that comes with following God can take a while. Along the way are ups and downs. Rarely do any of us get there on our own. God often puts special persons in our path to guide us along the worship/discipleship journey. Let's now take a look at the growing-healthy practices to notice in the leader story:

**When you must discontinue a service.** There is a lot of grief among church people when they must end a worship service because it is not growing. Grief is appropriate. Do not shove it under the carpet. Honor it and help people move on.

**The fix:** Start again, the right way. You need training and coaching. See the Additional Resources for references.

**Pruning.** The new pastor mentored and shaped the younger leader. In turn, the younger leader developed a stronger mentoring relationship with the music team.

**The fix:** Humility. Our story lead character has gone from angry, rebellious and maybe arrogant to open, serious (about his work) and moldable like a jar of clay. He had to do his own soul work to get to that place. One cannot will or fake humility. All leaders lead from their own place of authenticity.

**Involving new people.** Our protagonist was thinking about the guest that left (who is the lead protagonist in the Guest Experience stories). She would have been the kind of person who would have been an asset to a launch team (the group of people who start a new service in a new or existing church).

**The fix:** Let go of theological worries. Some leaders worry that people new to the faith do not have the theological depth to give input into worship service design and development. We recommend that you not worry about that too much. You, as leaders, will bring the theological depth. New people teach church people about God and many times have a better feel for seekers. New people help us with relevance.

 **CONSTRUCTION TIME**
**GO TO THE WORKBOOK, Part Two, Chapter Eight, Phase Four**

Our *Leader Experience* story opens the door to a discussion on worship design and sermon writing teams. For further technical development on each, head to the Workbook!

# Chapter Nine _____

## Phase Five:  Artistry

The worship service is a place of tremendous artistic and creative opportunity. Ah, but what is art? Has anyone ever gone to an art museum and looked at a modern painting they did not understand and said, "My nine-year-old could do better than that?" But there is that painting, hanging in the museum.

Cathy's friend Mary is a docent at the Minneapolis Institute of Arts. Mary shared a definition of art from the curator of the Minnesota Artists Exhibition Program: *a body of work with a clarity of intent.* That which we perceive to be art does not make it art; the clarity of intent of the body of work is what makes it art. This book is art. The meal you prepared for your spouse last Valentine's day was art. The raising of your child is art. Your hard work to have a healthy marriage is art.

Your worship service is art – even if some people do not like the service. It is still art because it is a body of work with a clarity of intent. Ah, but what is your intent? And does your art fulfill the intent that you have established? That is the part we could judge with esoteric discussions into the wee hours of the morning. Remember, artistry is a fundamental component in your worship bridge. It is one of the trusses!

Fruit is the obvious clue as to whether your worship service is fulfilling its intent. The fruit is people, both old and new, are coming to that service and growing as disciples who exhibit transformed lives. The fruit also shows up when disciples are discipling new people. Not everyone who ever attends your worship service will like what you do. But many must like it and relate to it to be transformed by it and fulfill the purpose you set out to fulfill. That purpose is to make new disciples of Jesus Christ for the transformation of the world. At least, we hope that is your intent. It is our intent to help you fulfill that specific intent. We hope we have helped in some small and maybe even large way with our art.

## Transitions: *the focus of this chapter*

In the public worship venue, it is important to communicate the intent of the service so that we can fulfill it. We are gathered to praise God and encourage discipleship. It is no secret; we want everyone to know it. We communicate that intent overtly and subtly in numerous ways many of which we have already shared.

One way the intent of the service is communicated to persons in seats is through the leadership of the upfront leader. We have spoken of this role throughout *Building Worship Bridges*. A specific way the upfront leader guides the congregation is through transitions. We have not yet spoken about transitions. Transitions are a part of artistry, and artistry is one of the trusses on our worship bridge.

Transitions are like glue. They connect one part of the service to the next. For example, The Welcome (mentioned frequently in previous chapters) is a transition between the Praise and the Proclamation. Music can also transition between segments or within one segment. Doing transitions well creates good flow in the worship service.

We do not do transitions well in most of our worship services. They are clunky and distracting, proving that most of us in worship leadership do not understand how important they are. On a technical level, transitions allow worship leaders to guide groups of people over 50 in number through a collective experience. Simultaneously on a spiritual level, transitions allow individuals in that group to respond to God in their own way, internally, apart from the group they are worshiping with. Worship with excellent transitions is experienced as one continuous, connected experience. Worship without good transitions feels like there are all sorts of stops and starts. Poor transitions

134

often leave the participant feeling portions of the experience are disconnected from the other.

## THE BIBLICAL THEME OF ARTISTRY:
### God's Transformational Power

Transitions are part of God's art and God is the ultimate artist. God created beautiful humanity as part of creation. God created us to be in relationship with God through worship. Worshiping God transforms us when we transition our relationship with God from superficial to personal, or from sinner to redeemed sinner (for example). When humans interact with God's artistry, we receive God's power and we are transformed by that power. **Transformation is the ultimate transition.**

In the public gathering, God's power is also available because we are interacting with God's artistry of worship. In all aspects of the service, we find God's power. We have spent the previous four chapters identifying the ways in which persons in seats interact with God's power in public space.

Transformation can occur any time when persons in seats respond to what is going on around them internally and transition their thinking about God (hopefully in a positive direction!).

Persons in seats need corporate content during the public gathering to lead them to the internal, individual, mental, spiritual transitions. The content that most often brings transformation is God's story and their story - our story intertwining. Sometimes God's and our stories connect through liturgies or music. Sometimes they connect through confession or prayer. Sometimes the story of God connecting with our story comes through the overall ebb and flow of the service ... technical transitions.

### Receiving God's power

It is very, very – yes very – difficult to teach worship leadership. But that is what we are attempting. Teaching is art. The way in which a worship leader can lead is art. If a leader can sense what is going on in the room spiritually and shares it spontaneously – (in words, music, or even silence) persons in seats might not get it. Or they might. The only measure anyone has of the impact of their worship leading art is fruit.

Persons in seats will come back and bring their friends when they receive God's power in public space – power they cannot receive anywhere else.

Bishop Farr raises the question of communicating clarity of intent in non-artsy terms. Have you ever wondered why so many more people show up on Christmas and Easter than any other worship services of the year? We Christians chalk it up to family obligations or cultural expectations. Bishop Farr wonders if people continue to attend only on our two most high Holy Days hoping that this time it would matter, that they might experience something. For the most part, they walk away wanting. So, they do not come back until next year. The God-sized hole might lead them back to give us or another church one more chance.

Blogger Carey Nieuwhof says something similar to Bishop Farr. In a blog from Easter 2014, he says that many Creaster worshipers (Christmas and Easter only) don't make a connection on Christmas and Easter. He says most preachers and worship leaders reiterate the story; but the guest already knows the story. What they don't know is the relevance.[34]

In Chapter One, we said to tell God's story and your story to impact worship design. Then we suggested we pay attention to first impressions and quality. Then we promoted energy for the first ten minutes and for your own spiritual practices. Next, we focused on discipleship through a strong worship ending and behind the scenes planning. Right now, without going a step further, you have the makings of a good worship service.

But something is still missing. It is not the story; it is the

---

[34] Carey Nieuwhof, Why Some Unchurched People Don't Connect with East-er http://careynieuwhof.com/2014/04/easter-unchurched/

power of the story. That is what artistry brings into the worship service through the skillful use of transitions. In someone's mind in public space there is a still small voice he hears:

*God spoke to you out of the fire. You heard the sound of words but you saw nothing - no form, only a voice.*

**Deuteronomy 4:12, (MSG)**

Listen...

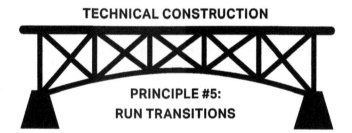

**TECHNICAL CONSTRUCTION**

**PRINCIPLE #5:**
**RUN TRANSITIONS**

Here are some examples of transitions affecting the worshiper, some of which we have already discussed:

- From one part of the basic worship format to the next with grace.
- From the beginning of worship to the end
- From the beginning of each segment of the service to the end of that segment
- From a person's front door to the front door of the church
- From the front door of the church to the start of the worship service
- From the worship service back out into the world at the end
- From a heart of disappointment to a heart of hope
- From an attitude of rebellion to an attitude of trust

We will discuss many more transitions in the Workbook.

*Learn to run transitions technically*
*to lead them spiritually.*

## PREPARE YOUR CHURCH FOR GUESTS: *The Art*

Transitions in a worship service are a body of work that God intends to use for impact upon persons in seats. When worship leaders come to the public worship service spiritually ready to hear God's voice, they often will gain a sense of the presence of God. Sensing God causes them to want to share God's presence with persons in seats, because they have noticed it. Speaking about what they see and hear or leading a congregation into silence or singing a verse of a song without accompaniment can be more real than reality TV! It is a collective experience that individuals are responding to.

## THE GUEST EXPERIENCE: *Can't stop the feeling* [35]

Transitions communicate volumes to your congregation about your church. They communicate if you are casual, formal, relational, reserved, prepared or unprepared. What do you want your guest to know about you? It is real to plan for it. Guests will take the positive experience home with them.

### A guest's experience

*The week after you went to Accelerating Church, you found your-self thinking about how casual everything seemed. The chick upfront*

---

[35] Cathy feels compelled to give a shout out to Justin Timberlake's 2016 song and video, Can't Stop the Feeling. Head to YouTube to see both versions of the vid for some fun and encouragement. You will be hum-ming the tune for days. That is how worship should be when we leave the worship service to return to our own daily lives.

*was sort of dressed like you. You actually kind of felt overdressed. Even though it was laid back the service just flew by.*

*Perhaps it was because you had gone to Decelerating Church that morning before you went to Accelerating Church that you noticed so many things about Accelerating Church by comparison. You could not get your mind off the guy that met you at the door at Accelerating Church who made you feel so comfortable even though you walked in late. Even the parking lot people were fun. And then, the conversation you had with the welcomer chick after the service was so great. She was really, really nice. She introduced you to the guy that was getting the fasting group together. You were close to joining it, but you weren't quite ready. You did plan to come back next Sunday to hear about what people experienced. He suggested you follow him on Twitter to hear about some fasting ups and downs, from him and other participants.*

*A few days later at work, you were having lunch with a single guy from another department that you kind of liked. He never seemed like a partier to you so you never gave him much attention before. He never seemed judgmental either about you having two kids with different dads. You wondered if maybe you were a little older than him. You figured he hadn't given you much thought before because you were probably too opposite of him. You wondered if he maybe had a story, too, that would make your story seem tame. Probably not. He seemed stable. But you never know.*

*You were thinking it was time you changed your circle of friends. So, when you saw him sitting alone at lunch, you went and sat by him. He smiled when you came over. As you chatted, you heard the words coming out of your mouth about the church experience you had that last weekend. You hadn't intended to say any of that and now here you were. The big shocker is that you asked him if he'd ever want to come with you. He said maybe, then he teased you about asking him on a date to CHURCH of all places. Then he told you he goes to that church sometimes. Wow!*

139

We notice transitions in the worship service when they are not done well. When they are done with artistry, they bring power to the worship experience. The power is below the surface. It impacts us in ways we do not plan for even with planned transitions. Let's take a look at some highlights of the guest's story:

**A casual atmosphere.** Have you noticed most restaurants these days do not have a dress code? Our current culture is decidedly less formal than it was even earlier in the 21st Century. It's important to insert some casual vibe into the way you do things in church, too.

 **The fix: Address the dress code.** We introduced the role of the host earlier. Your host introduces cultural relevance. She underscores the casual atmosphere because he speaks directly to the congregation and you are "in her living room." She (or he) comes off approachable and relatable. The casual welcome is an important juxtaposition to high tech, too. If your service is a liturgy driven, very traditional service, developing the role of the host will give persons in seats a different view of you (especially if the pastor and the choir wear robes). At the least, the host should dress like the mission field. Some might argue that the pastor probably should, too!

**A sense of ambiance.** The worship service should have some atmosphere. If you do not know what that is, think the opposite: stark or sterile. Sterility is what you find in a shopping mall with bright lights shining from overhead. The lights seem to make everything feel disconnected. Perhaps that is so you will concentrate on your shopping.

 **The fix:** Focus on relationships. The host in our guest experience stories is relational. The connector and the greeters were relational. The experience after the service is relational. Relationships are bridge builders. They are part of creating ambience and thus strong transitions.

**Blending in.** We mentioned this in Chapter Six where we introduced the idea that lighting might have something to do with helping guests not feel exposed.

**The fix:** Manage your lighting with what you have. Next look at what it will take to upgrade and develop a plan. A darker room during the opening praise allows people to fold into the experience much more comfortably than if the room is very bright. It also helps them connect deep inside themselves. Brighter lights work better for the sermon, especially if you want persons in seats to take notes. If you are in an older building, chances are your sanctuary lighting is stark and perhaps not very easy to manage since there is no dimmer. In that case, create a prayer time and turn off and turn on lights during it. See charts in the workbook for how to use prayer as a transition tool.

### ADAPTIVE CONSTRUCTION

**PRINCIPLE #5:
RUN YOUR RACE**

*24 You've all been to the stadium and seen the athletes race. Everyone runs; one wins. Run to win. 25 All good athletes train hard. They do it for a gold medal that tarnishes and fades. You're after one that's gold eternally. 26 I don't know about you, but I'm running hard for the finish line. I'm giving it everything I've got. No sloppy living for me! 27 I'm staying alert and in top condition. I'm not going to get caught napping, telling everyone else all about it and then missing out myself.*

**1 Corinthians 9: 24 – 27 (MSG)**

What is the power of God's story in your life? What is the power of your story? What is the impact of God's love of people upon you and upon your ability to welcome new people into an existing environment? What is the impact of your own devotion to quality? What is the excitement you feel over praising God in the public space especially at the beginning of your service? What is the excitement you feel of spending time alone with God and hearing God's voice for the first time that day? What do you gain from leading persons in seats into the presence of Christ? What do you gain from surrendering to God so that you can be present to persons in seats? Repeat asking these questions often.

The "repeat" can be demanding and thus tiring for vocational worship leaders. It is a tiring role because Sunday follows Sunday follows Sunday, and infinitum. We balance the demands of upfront leadership with perseverance. We burn out when we do not take the time to further our own personal relationship with God and Christian community.

## PREPARE YOURSELF FOR GUESTS: *Believe!*

We have taken you through many technical and adaptive changes to get us near to the end of our story. In Christianity, the end is always the beginning. We trust that the end of this material affords you a boost of energy and commitment to reboot your leadership role yet again. God has called you to your work. But first God has called you to follow Christ. We are public worship leaders second. We are Christ followers first. The energy to persevere comes from that foundational belief.

## THE LEADER EXPERIENCE: *The Artist*

The worship leader experience and the guest experience should dovetail if the guest is going to make a connection. When the artist that leads the worship service practices the presence of

Christ, worship leaders cross paths with persons in seats.

## A leader's experience

*The most significant change in your life in the past six months is the amount of time you are spending with your friends. This is probably because of your new girlfriend. You'd hang out as couples eating out and having game nights and other stuff. Just talking sometimes. You have lots of discussions about faith. Some of the friends have started coming to your service. They often mention it's interesting to hear things you said to them the night before coming out in the service.*

*One day your girlfriend told you about this woman she had become friends with at work. They had gotten to talking and the woman told her she had been to your church and it was terrible! You asked your girlfriend what the woman looked like. Your girlfriend was stunned that you knew who the woman was. You laughed about it. Your girlfriend said that woman was super involved at Accelerating Church. Figures. You were okay with it though. As you looked out at the group of people there that Sunday, you knew how different it was from so many months ago when that guest dropped in and left.*

*Everyone at the service now wanted to be there.*

## LEADER EXPERIENCE DEBRIEF: *Integration*

If we are authentic leaders in our present-day culture, then our own lives and our lives of worship should connect. Integrating everyday life with church life is transitional. Let's now take a look at the highlights in the leader story:

**Having fun.** Part of the transitional environment of worship is when it is fun. We have been serious through the pages of our book. Powerful worship is serious. And, it is fun.

**The fix:** Love what you do. Don't settle for mediocrity.

**Inviting your friends.** Too many of us clergy and worship leader types do not have much of a social life.

**The fix:** Date night!

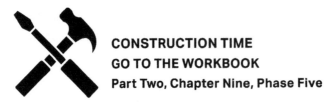

**CONSTRUCTION TIME**
**GO TO THE WORKBOOK**
**Part Two, Chapter Nine, Phase Five**

As we told you earlier, we will delve into many ways to transition your service through technical aspects of transitions. We'll use prayer, lighting, sitting, standing, and speaking. You will see how to run a worship service from beginning to end, with powerful transitions.

# The Ten Phases

**for**
**Building Worship Bridges**

| TECHNICAL | ADAPTIVE |
|:---:|:---:|
| Tell God's Story | Tell Your Story |
| Pay Attention to First Impressions | Pay Attention to Quality |
| Enliven the First Ten Minute | Enliven Spiritual Practices |
| Strengthen the Ending | Strengthen Design Processes |
| Run Transitions | Run the Race |

# Epilogue _____

*You and that worship leader's girlfriend were good work friends. She invited you to come back to the church you had tried that one morning and you thought you might some time. But you loved Accelerating Church and you had lots of friends there. You were going to be baptized there this morning with your kids. Your boyfriend from work was meeting you there with his parents. You had to drive past the church that was once decelerating to go pick up your mom.*

*Even though you knew they were doing much better from your friend at work, you were still surprised to see so many cars out in front. Just as you were about to pass by, you saw a truck you recognized pull into the parking lot. You noticed the driver, but he didn't see you. It was a guy you used to hang out with ... kind of an old boyfriend. You would have never thought he'd be in church. Your work friend wasn't lying when she said things were going better. You felt good for them.*

# Afterword _____

At the very beginning of *Building Worship Bridges*, Cathy Townley, Kay Kotan and Bishop Farr stated that in most Mainline churches in America, "...the worship bridge is broken." They're right.

In my work as the President of Faith Perceptions (research company that started in 2008 to give churches an unbiased opinion on their worship services from persons outside the church) I, along with my team, have gathered data from thousands of people that churches say they want to reach out to, who have no current church connection. Faith Perceptions refers to this process as The Mystery Guest Program. We have worked extensively with the Healthy Church Initiative (HCI), helping the churches they work with gain an outside perspective so that the churches can improve the way they engage and connect with their first-time guests.

In our research, a significant finding is that new people do not see our churches' worship services the way we in the church see them. Hospitality, kids and music (the Three Big Wows, as Cathy, Kay and Bishop Farr referred to them) usually miss the mark, as does the entire worship experience. Our Mystery Guest reports reveal a disconnect:

> *"In churches, I sometimes get that feeling during worship that the congregation just goes through the motions instead of approaching worship with this attitude that says, "We were made for this, so let's worship God with all we've got."*
> **– Church Guest**

Initially we believed the guest wasn't connecting with the worship style the church offered – that a style "disconnect" and lack of excellence were the primary reasons the guest did not want to return to that service. We were wrong. We have found

149

that style and excellence are still important, but we have also found that authenticity is even more important. Cathy, Kay and Bishop Farr purposefully conveyed that worship must be real and excellent simultaneously. Churches can engage in many different styles of worship, but the motive and sincerity behind the worship are what most matter, as this comment from a Mystery Guest report shows us:

> *"The music was mostly traditional which typically isn't my favorite form of music, but the energy and engagement of the congregation really made it enjoyable. I felt like these people really believed what they were singing!"*
> **– Church Guest**

Chuck Swindoll once said there is no such thing as seekers in the church; only watchers. People don't come to church convinced that there is hope. As Cathy, Kay and Bishop Farr alluded to in their writing, new people are watching you, looking for evidence that you yourself have found hope. When guests observe lifeless, unengaging worship in your church, they will not believe the words you use to say that God has changed you.

Emmanuel Cleaver II, a United Methodist Pastor and a member of the United States House of Representatives said, "The message we preach doesn't have to change, but how we deliver it can." In *Building Worship Bridges*, Cathy, Kay and Bishop Farr did not tell you to compromise God's truths as you understand them. The message they did convey, however, is that we as the church must translate that truth to today, by being less focused on preserving our heritage and our traditions and more concerned about meeting people where they are. Faith Perceptions concurs.

In our Mystery Guest report, we always ask the mystery guest if they'll come back to your church. You can learn something about your worship service by asking similar questions of yourselves:

How many new people attended our church in the past year? How many never came back?

Faith Perception's research shows us that if your worship service is bland and unengaging, your guest will not be back, since you have not shown them your hope through the act of praising God. Faith Perceptions prays you learn how to share the promise of transformation with your guests through your public praise in the worship service. *Building Worship Bridges* has given you the tools to do so.

**Melanie Smollen, President**
FaithPerceptions.com

# Other books from
# Market Square Books

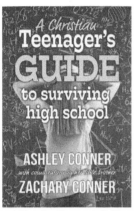

**A Christian Teenager's Guide
To Surviving High School**
Ashley Conner & Zachary Conner

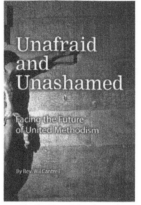

**Unafraid and Unashamed**
*Facing the Future of United Methodism*
Wil Cantrell

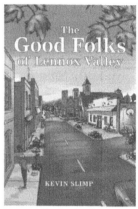

**The Good Folks
of Lennox Valley**
Kevin Slimp

**Understanding Your Call**
Through the Eyes of 11 Biblical Figures

**Understanding Your Call**
Contributors

Rev. Wil Cantrell

Rev. Rob Couch

Bishop Bob Farr

Rev. Aleze Fulbright

Rev. Larry Ousley

Rev. Jacob Reedy

Kevin Slimp

Bishop Debbie Wallace-Padgett

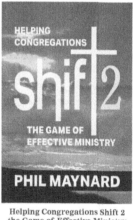

**Helping Congregations Shift 2
the Game of Effective Ministry**
Phil Maynard

## marketsquarebooks.com